Topics
for Today

Third Edition

Reading For Today SERIES, BOOK 5

LORRAINE C. SMITH
Adelphi University

NANCY NICI MARE
English Language Institute
Queens College
The City University of New York

THOMSON
™
HEINLE

Australia • Canada • Mexico • Singapore • United Kingdom • United States

THOMSON
HEINLE

Topics for Today, Third Edition
Lorraine C. Smith and Nancy Nici Mare

Publisher, Adult and Academic ESL: *James W. Brown*
Senior Acquisitions Editor: *Sherrise Roehr*
Director of Development: *Anita Raducanu*
Development Editor: *Sarah Barnicle*
Assistant Editor: *Audra Longert*
Editorial Assistant: *Katherine Reilly*
Editorial Intern: *Sarah Bilodeau*
Senior Production Editor: *Maryellen E. Killeen*
Director of Marketing: *Amy Mabley*
Director, Global ESL Training & Development:
  Evelyn Nelson

Senior Print Buyer: *Mary Beth Hennebury*
Contributing Writer: *Barbara Gaffney*
Compositor: *Parkwood Composition Service*
Project Manager: *Hockett Editorial Service*
Photo Researcher: *Susan Van Etten*
Photography Manager: *Sheri Blaney*
Illustrator: *Glenn Reid*
Cover Designer: *Ha Ngyuen*
Text Designer: *Carole Rollins*
Printer: *Quebecor World*

Printed in the United States of America
1 2 3 4 5 6 7 8 9 10   06 05 04

For permission to use material from this text or product submit a request online at www.thomson.com

For more information contact Heinle, 25 Thomson Place, Boston, Massachusetts 02210 USA, or you can visit our Internet site at http://www.heinle.com

Library of Congress Control Number   2003110885

ISBN 1-4130-0811-9
ISE ISBN   1-4130-0076-2

To Elizabeth

CONTENTS

Unit and Chapter Readings	Reading Skills Focus	Follow-up Skills Focus and Activities
Unit 2 **Influences on Our Lives: Nature Versus Nurture** Chapter 4 **Who Lives Longer?** *Page 76* Another Perspective: **More Senior Citizens, Fewer Kids** *Page 88*	• Preview reading through the title and a group activity to activate background knowledge • Identify and paraphrase the main idea • Identify & organize details of reading in chart form • Analyze reading through true/false/not mentioned, multiple choice, and short answer questions • Use context clues to understand vocabulary and select synonyms • Read dictionary entries to select accurate definitions • Learn about and improve personal reading strategies	• *Critical Thinking:* Infer information from the text; Identify the author's tone; Support answers with examples; Draw conclusions from the reading; Interpret a line graph; Interpret statistics from a chart • *Speaking and Discussion:* Develop and report on ideas with a group; Agree and disagree with the opinions of others • *Writing:* Write a summary from notes; Design a survey; Write a composition from information found in chart form; Write a journal entry
Chapter 5 **The Mindset of Health** *Page 97* Another Perspective: **How to Behave in a Hospital** *Page 111*	• Preview reading by examining photographs, through a group discussion, and by considering the title • Identify and paraphrase the main idea • Identify & organize details in a flowchart form • Analyze reading through true/false/inference, multiple choice, and short answer questions • Use context clues to understand vocabulary and select synonyms • Read dictionary entries to select accurate definitions • Learn about and improve personal reading strategies	• *Critical Thinking:* Infer information from the text; Agree or disagree with author, supporting ideas with examples; Draw conclusions; Identify effects • *Speaking and Discussion:* Discuss hypothetical situations; Role play; Compare answers with the opinions of others • *Writing:* Make lists with a group; Write a summary from flowchart notes; Write a journal entry
Chapter 6 **Small Wonders** *Page 118* Another Perspective: **Reading at 8 Months? That Was Just the Start** *Page 133*	• Preview reading through prereading questions to activate background knowledge • Identify and paraphrase the main idea • Identify & organize details in chart form • Analyze reading through true/false/inference, multiple choice, and short answer questions • Use context clues to understand vocabulary and select synonyms • Read dictionary entries to select accurate definitions • Learn about and improve personal reading strategies	• *Critical Thinking:* Make inferences about author comments; Support answers with examples; Identify problems and solutions; Draw conclusions • *Speaking and Discussion:* Conduct and report on a survey; Agree and disagree with the opinions of others • *Writing and Research:* Write a summary from notes; Write a journal entry; Write a list of questions; Research and summarize information about child prodigies • *Listening and Viewing:* **CNN® Video Report:** **Michael Kearney, Child Prodigy** • *Viewing and Research:* **InfoTrac® Search:** **Men, Women, and Longevity**

SKILLS

Unit and Chapter Readings	Reading Skills Focus	Follow-up Skills Focus and Activities
Unit 3 **Technology and Ethical Issues** Chapter 7 **Assisted Suicide: Multiple Perspectives** *Page 146* Another Perspective: **Should Doctors Be Allowed to Help Terminally Ill Patients Commit Suicide?** *Page 160*	• Preview reading through title and prereading questions to activate background knowledge • Identify and paraphrase the main idea • Identify & organize details in a flowchart • Analyze reading through true/false/inference, multiple choice, and short answer questions • Use context clues to understand vocabulary and select synonyms • Read dictionary entries to select accurate definitions • Learn about and improve personal reading strategies	• *Critical Thinking:* Compare similarities and differences; Compare points of view; Infer information from the text; Support answers with examples; Draw conclusions • *Speaking and Discussion:* Conduct and report on a survey; Create a committee to discuss ethics and consequences; Agree and disagree with the opinions of others • *Writing:* Make and compare lists; Write a summary from flowchart notes; Write an opinion composition; Write a journal entry
Chapter 8 **Trading Flesh around the Globe** *Page 167* **Sales of Kidneys Prompt New Laws and Debate** *Page 169*	• Prepare for main reading by reading title and introductory reading, taking a survey, and answering prereading questions • Identify & paraphrase the main idea • Identify & organize details in a chart • Analyze reading through true/false/not mentioned, multiple choice, and short answer questions • Use context clues to understand vocabulary and select synonyms • Read dictionary entries to select accurate definitions • Learn about and improve personal reading strategies	• *Critical Thinking:* Infer information from the text; Support answers with reasons and examples; Draw conclusions; Understand a bar graph; Prioritize a list • *Speaking and Discussion:* Compare priorities; Share and discuss opinions; Discuss causes for transplantation debate • *Writing:* Write a summary from notes in chart; Write a personal position and/or opinion composition; Write a journal entry
Chapter 9 **The Gift of Life: When One Body Can Save Another** *Page 188* Another Perspective: **Two Parents Offer Their Daughter the Breath of Life—to No Avail** *Page 203*	• Preview reading through title, introductory reading, and prereading questions to activate background knowledge • Identify and paraphrase the main idea • Identify & organize details in a flowchart • Analyze reading through true/false/inference, multiple choice, and short answer questions • Use context clues to understand vocabulary and select synonyms • Read dictionary entries to select accurate definitions • Learn about and improve personal reading strategies	• *Critical Thinking:* Infer information from the text; Support answers with examples; Draw conclusions • *Speaking and Discussion:* Agree or disagree with medical decisions; Conduct a survey and discuss results • *Writing:* Write a summary from flowchart notes; Write a position letter; Write a paragraph about organ donation; Write a journal entry voicing your opinion • *Listening and Viewing:* **CNN® Video Report:** **Baby Donor** • Viewing and Research: **InfoTrac® Search:** **Organs for Sale**

x   Skills

SKILLS

PREFACE

Topics for Today, Third Edition, is an ESL/EFL reading skills text intended for advanced, college-bound students. The passages in this book are original articles from periodicals and newspapers. Some have been shortened slightly, but none have been simplified; consequently, students have the opportunity to read actual selections from a variety of publications. The topics are fresh and timely. The issues are global in nature. Experience has shown that college-bound students are interested in modern topics of a more academic nature than is often found in ESL/EFL texts. They need extensive reading in the styles of writing and the vocabulary that they will actually encounter during their university studies. This book provides them with this essential practice. It requires students to not only read an article, but also to extract information from various forms of charts, graphs, and illustrations.

Topics for Today, Third Edition, is one in a series of reading skills texts. The complete series has been designed to meet the needs of students from the beginning to the advanced levels and includes the following:

- *Themes for Today*   beginning
- *Insights for Today*   high beginning
- *Issues for Today*   intermediate
- *Concepts for Today*   high intermediate
- *Topics for Today*   advanced

Topics for Today, Third Edition, has been designed for flexible use by teachers and students. The text consists of four units, each containing three chapters that deal with related subjects. Each chapter includes a second reading that relates to the topic of the main reading, and provides another perspective on the subject matter of that chapter. At the same time, each chapter is entirely separate in content from the other chapters contained in that unit. This approach gives teachers and students the option of either completing all three chapters in a unit, in any order they wish, or of choosing individual chapters as a focus in class.

The prereading preparation before each reading helps activate the students' background knowledge of the topic and encourages students to think about the ideas, facts, and vocabulary that will be presented. The exercises and activities that follow the reading passage are intended to develop and improve vital skills, including identifying main idea and supporting details, summary writing, overall reading proficiency, inferencing ability, learning vocabulary from context, using the dictionary appropriately, and critical thinking. The activities give students the opportunity to master useful vocabulary encountered in the articles through discussion and group work and lead the students through general comprehension of main ideas and specific information. Equally important, the text provides the students with regular opportunities to reflect on how the reading strategies they use helps them improve their overall reading proficiency.

As the students interact with the text, they will improve their skills and develop confidence in their ability to understand new material. At the same time, they and their teacher will be able to observe their steady progress towards skillful, independent reading.

New to the Third Edition

While *Topics for Today, Third Edition,* retains the overall format of the second edition, the authors have made several significant changes. *Topics for Today, Third Edition,* comprises twelve chapters, three chapters in each of four units. The third edition contains two new chapters: "Hop, Skip . . . and Software?" about children and computers, and "Small Wonders" about child prodigies. These revisions have been designed to provide students with extensive reading practice on contemporary topics.

The third edition includes new photographs and graphics, which are designed both to enhance students' comprehension of information processed in graphs and to facilitate understanding of the text they relate to.

In addition to the new chapters, the third edition is now accompanied by a CNN® video composed of video clips chosen to complement the theme and vocabulary of one of the chapters in each unit. At the end of each unit, video activities accompany the video to assist students in their viewing comprehension. Also new to *Topics for Today, Third Edition,* are InfoTrac® online activities designed to encourage students with school or home access to use the Internet to research in depth about a topic they read about in the text.

All of these revisions and enhancements for *Topics for Today, Third Edition,* have been designed to help students improve their reading skills, to develop confidence as they work through the text, and to prepare them for academic work and the electronic world of information they are about to encounter.

INTRODUCTION

How to Use This Book

Every chapter in this book consists of the following:

Prereading Preparation
Reading Passages
Reading Overview: Main Idea, Details, and Summary
Statement Evaluation
Reading Analysis
Dictionary Skills
Critical Thinking
Another Perspective
Follow-up Activities
Topics for Discussion and Writing
Cloze Quiz

The second reading in each chapter (Another Perspective) may be part of the Prereading Preparation in order to provide background knowledge for the main reading of the chapter or to provide the readers with the opportunity to consider certain perspectives on the main reading. The second reading may also be found later in the chapter, where it provides another perspective on the topic of the main reading.

There is a crossword puzzle, as well as CNN® video activities, and InfoTrac Online Library research activities at the end of each unit. An Index of Key Words and Phrases and Skills Index are located at the end of the book.

The format of each chapter in the book is consistent. Some activities, by their nature, involve pair and group work. Other exercises may be assigned for homework. This choice, of course, depends on the individual teacher's preference, as well as the availability of class time.

Prereading Preparation

The prereading activities vary throughout the text, depending on the subject matter. This section is designed to stimulate student interest and generate vocabulary relevant to the passage. The students should consider the source of the article, relate the topic to their own experience, and try to predict what they are going to read about.

The Reading Passage

Research has demonstrated the value of multiple readings, especially where each reading serves a specific purpose. The students will read each passage several times. As the students read the passage for the first time, for example, they should be encouraged to identify main ideas. During the second reading, they will identify supporting details. At the third reading, students can focus on unfamiliar vocabulary as they work through the Reading Analysis and Dictionary Skills.

Reading Overview: Main Idea, Details, and Summary

In this exercise, students are asked to read the passage a second time and take notes based in part on the main ideas they identified during their first reading. The teacher may want to review the concept of main idea, notetaking, and summarizing before beginning the exercise. The Details outline, chart, or flowchart can be sketched by the teacher on the blackboard and completed by individual students in front of the class. Variations can be discussed by the class as a group. It should be pointed out to the students that in American colleges, teachers often base their exams on the notes that the students are expected to take during class lectures. When the students have finished notetaking, they are asked to briefly summarize the passage.

Statement Evaluation

After reading, taking notes, and summarizing the passage, the students will read a series of statements and check whether each is true, false, an opinion, an inference, or not mentioned in the reading. This activity can be done individually or in pairs. Students should be encouraged to discuss their responses.

Reading Analysis

The students will read each question and answer it. This exercise deals with vocabulary from context, transition words, punctuation clues, sentence structure, and sentence comprehension. It may be helpful for students to read the passage again as they work on this exercise. The Reading Analysis exercise is effective when done in pairs because students have an opportunity to discuss their responses.

Dictionary Skills

The entries in this section have been taken from *Merriam-Webster's Collegiate On-line Dictionary* © 2002. This exercise provides the students with much needed practice in selecting the appropriate dictionary entry for an unknown word. The students are given an authentic dictionary entry for one of the words in the text. One or more sentences containing the unknown word are provided above the entry. The student reads the entry and selects the appropriate one, given the context provided. Students need to understand that this is not always a clear process; some entries are very similar, and it could be that more than one entry is appropriate if the context is general. They should aim for the nearest in meaning rather than absolute correctness. The students can work in pairs on this exercise and report back to the class. They should be prepared to justify their choice.

Critical Thinking

For this activity, the students refer back to parts of the article, think about the implications of the information or comments that are contained, and consider the author's purpose and tone. The goal of the exercise is for students to form their own ideas and opinions on aspects of the topic discussed. The students can work on these questions as an individual writing exercise or orally as a small group discussion activity. In this activity, students are encouraged to use the vocabulary they have been learning.

Another Perspective

The second reading in the chapters provides another point of view, or an additional topic, related to the main reading. The students should focus on general comprehension, on relating this reading to the primary reading, and on considering the ideas and information as they engage in the Follow-up Activities and Topics for Discussion and Writing.

Follow-up Activities

The first item in the Follow-up Activities is a *Self-Evaluation of Reading Strategies.* The purpose of this self-evaluation is to help students become more aware of the strategies they use to help themselves understand written material. It is a personal, reflective activity, and progress should be judged by the students themselves. At the same time, students should be encouraged to utilize these strategies in all their reading.

The remainder of each section contains a variety of activities, some intended for in-class work, others as out-of-class assignments. Some activities are designed for pair and small group work. Students are encouraged to use the information and vocabulary from the passages both orally and in writing.

Topics for Discussion and Writing

In this section, students are encouraged to use the information and vocabulary from the passage both orally and in writing. The writing assignments may be done entirely in class, begun in class and finished at home, or done at home. The last activity in this section is a journal-writing assignment that provides the students with an opportunity to reflect on the topic in the chapter and respond to it in some personal way. Students should be encouraged to keep a journal, and to write in it regularly. The students' journal writing may be purely personal, or the students may choose to have the teacher read them. The teacher may wish to respond to the students' journal entries, but not to correct them.

Cloze Quiz

The Cloze Quiz in each chapter serves as a final review of the primary reading. By using a section of the chapter reading, Cloze exercises help students understand that they can select the missing word by looking closely at the context. For a variation on this exercise, have students block the vocabulary words at the top of the quiz and ask them to offer other words that might help complete the sentences in a meaningful way. Students can work on the quizzes alone, and then compare their answers with a partner, or they may do the quizzes alone and have the instructor check their responses.

Crossword Puzzle

The crossword puzzles are located at the end of each unit. They provide a review of the vocabulary in the chapters in the given unit. They may be done in pairs, as a homework assignment, or as an optional enrichment activity.

CNN® Video Report and InfoTrac® Online Library Research Activities

At the end of each unit are optional video and InfoTrac Internet activities designed to accompany one of the chapter topics presented in each unit. Authentic CNN videos were chosen to continue ideas presented in the readings, to reinforce vocabulary learned, and to encourage individual interest as well as group discussion. The optional InfoTrac activities are provided to encourage students to explore information learned in *Topics for Today, Third Edition,* through an online research library available to them at school, in the library, or at home.

Index of Key Words and Phrases

This section contains important words and phrases from all the chapters for easy reference. It is located after the last chapter.

ACKNOWLEDGMENTS

We are grateful to everyone at Heinle, especially to Sherrise Roehr for her continued support, to Sarah Barnicle for her keen eye and untiring efforts, and to Maryellen Killeen for her hard work. Special thanks also go to Rachel Youngman of Hockett Editorial Service for her diligence. As always, we are appreciative of the ongoing encouragement from our family and friends.

L.C.S. and N.N.M.

UNIT 1

SOCIETY: SCHOOL AND FAMILY

1

Hop, Skip . . . and Software?

Prereading Preparation

1. Look at the picture and read the title of the chapter. What do you think the title means?

2. Do you think elementary school students should use computers in their classes? Work in a small group. Make a list of reasons for and against computer use in elementary school. Use the chart below to organize your ideas.

Should elementary school students use computers in their classrooms?	
Yes, because . . .	No, because . . .

3. At what age do you think children should start learning to use the computer? Discuss this question with your classmates.

Hop, Skip . . . and Software?

by Victoria Irwin
Christian Science Monitor

Jody Spanglet's seventh- and eighth-grade students at Charlottesville Waldorf School in Virginia are studying revolutions. They dissect the Declaration of Independence, delve into the French rebellion against Louis XIV, and read about the various inventors who sparked the Industrial Revolution. But this study happens to be profoundly counterrevolutionary in today's cyber age: Not a single classroom in the school—from kindergarten through eighth grade—contains a computer.

Contrast that with the B.F. Yancey Elementary School in the southwest corner of the same county, Albemarle, in central Virginia. Here, computers are considered a rich resource and are used everywhere, from kindergarten through fifth grade. Third-graders working on oral history projects, for example, must first pass an online minicourse. They can then take home digital video cameras and download their oral history interviews onto the school computers, which are later made available on the school's website.

While the computerless Waldorf school is an exception in a nation that tends to embrace the technology revolution, both schools find themselves on the cutting edge of a debate about if and how computers should be introduced to children at the elementary-school level. At one end of the spectrum are coalitions such as the Alliance for Childhood, which has called for a moratorium on computers for students in early childhood and elementary schools. Concerns range from health issues to the need for stronger bonds between children and adults and more hands-on, active play in learning. At the other end are educators and technology enthusiasts, who believe that the use of computers at an early age—even when led by an adult—can open a child's mind to ideas and concepts that will kindle a great desire for learning, and perhaps make a child "smarter." Parents and guardians stand somewhere in the middle.

Many parents, who brag that their not-yet-3-year-old can type his or her name on a keyboard to enter a computer game, also admit to a grudging guilt that they did not instead send that same toddler outdoors to explore the wonders of blooming crocuses peeking through a layer of snow. "I don't think an elementary school virtually devoid of technology is necessarily bad," says Gene Maeroff, a professor at Columbia University's Teachers College and the author of "A Classroom of One: How Online Learning Is Changing Our Schools and Colleges." "Nor do I think a school loaded with technology is necessarily good, or better, at meeting students' needs," he says. "Computers can enhance education. But those possibilities become greater as kids get older, particularly at the secondary level, and absolutely at the college or postgraduate level."

Various studies show different effects of computer use in the classroom. In the late 1990s, the Educational Testing Service found that middle school students with well-trained teachers who used computers for "simulations and applications" in math class outperformed students on standardized tests who had not used them for that purpose. Meanwhile, eighth graders whose teachers used computers primarily for "drill and practice" performed even worse.

Born Digital

Computer technology is a fact of life in U.S. schools and homes. In the fall of 2000, 98 percent of public schools had access to the Internet in their schools, up from 35 percent six years earlier. And one in five students in public schools overall had access to a computer. In urban schools, that number drops to one in nine—which one technology advocate calls "not a digital divide, but a digital chasm." Today, according to the National Center for Educational Statistics, 80 percent of eighth-graders have access to a computer at home. Despite tightened state budgets, efforts are under way throughout the country to make technology even more relevant to students and learning. In Maine, every single seventh-grader (of whom there are slightly more than 18,000) has a laptop computer. In April, the state will begin sending computers to all eighth-graders, too. At Walton Middle School in Charlottesville, Va., seventh-graders are using what some predict will be the educational technology of the future—handheld computers—to facilitate writing.

But how computers are used varies greatly. Elliot Soloway, of the University of Michigan's Center for Highly Interactive Computing in Education, surveyed 4,000 schools last year and found that 65 percent of students in public schools, including high schools, spend less than 15 minutes a week using computers to access the Internet. *PC Magazine* reports that, of the $5 billion spent in the past decade to get computers into schools, 17 percent was used to educate teachers how to use the computers and integrate them into the curriculum. That gets to the heart of a debate over whether computer use in school is beneficial to students—or merely expensive window dressing.

Quality teachers have always worked toward finding many different paths to build basic knowledge and skills that students will need to succeed in school and life, says Becky Fisher, assistant director of the Department of Technology for the Albemarle County Schools. "Adding technology to the mix only makes a great teacher even better," she says. "The issue is not whether technology is appropriate for students—most kindergartners have already mastered more technology than existed when I was a child. Rather, it is whether our teachers are supported in a way to maximize the benefits of technology."

The Human Connection

Those who think technology in the classroom should wait see technology differently. "We strongly believe that actual experience is vital for young children," says Jody Spanglet of the Waldorf School in Charlottesville. "It is important for students to interact with one another, with teachers, and with the world—to explore ideas, participate in the creative process, and develop their knowledge, skills, abilities, and inner qualities." Nancy Regan, an administrator at the school, says: "A computer is a mediated experience. You touch the keyboard, but what happens online is not your doing. Our whole curriculum is based on human connection."

It is not that the Waldorf School eschews technology. For example, it has a website. And Ms. Regan says computers at the high school level are a good idea. Her seventh- and eighth-graders will soon be doing a report on inventors from the Industrial Revolution. To do so, they are required to use at least three resources, one of which can be the Internet. Kim McCormick, who has two daughters, ages 5 and 8, at the Charlottesville Waldorf School, says her family is not the least bit uncomfortable that their children's classrooms have no instructional computers. "We want them to get to know the world on a firsthand basis," says Ms. McCormick, a public school teacher. Her husband is a computer program analyst. "They see us using computers for work. But we don't have any kids' things on our computer. I have looked up butterflies for them before, so they know it can be a tool and resource. But they will learn to use a computer so quickly later. My husband, who works with computers for a living, didn't learn those skills until after college."

Going Online, Bit By Bit

Technology enthusiasts say computers should be introduced in stages. Paula White is a resource teacher for gifted students who helps integrate technology into the classroom at Yancey. White says that, at Yancey, while even kindergartners are using computers in the classroom—to count candy hearts on Valentine's Day, for instance—the teacher is the one entering the information. It is not as though children at Yancey are being plunked in front of a machine without interacting with teachers. But at some schools, lack of interaction is a real concern. A mother of three children in another Virginia elementary school says she is disappointed in the use of computers in two of her children's classes.

When they get computer time, it is usually in the morning or late afternoon, she says, when a teacher wants to grab some extra time at his or her desk.

110　　Bette Manchester of the Maine Learning Technology Initiative, which oversees the state's laptop project, says even the best teachers have a hard time incorporating the four or five desk computers that often sit in elementary classrooms. One-to-one computer access changes everything. "We've made this crystal clear: This is not about technology or software, it is about teaching kids," Ms. Manchester says. The success of the Maine program, she notes, depends

115　heavily on leadership among teachers in the state, as well as the complete integration of laptops into every school's curriculum. Training involves teachers, staff, students, and parents, and started well before the computers arrived. Manchester says middle school is a great time to give students intimate access to the technology. "They are at a critical stage developmentally," she says. "These

120　kids are learning how to learn, not simply reading to learn anymore. It's been very exciting watching them take off."

Reading Overview: Main Idea, Details, and Summary

Read the passage again. As you read, underline what you think are the most important ideas in the reading. Then, in one or two sentences, write the main idea of the reading. *Use your own words.*

Main Idea

_____

_____

_____

Details

Use the chart below to organize the details of the article. When you have finished, write a brief summary of the readings. *Use your own words.*

Name of School or Organization	Name of Spokesperson (if given)	What is this person or group's opinion about the use of computers in the classroom?
Charlottesville Waldorf School		
B.F. Yancey Elementary School		
The Alliance for Childhood		
Columbia University's Teachers College		
Education Testing Service		
The University of Michigan's Center for Highly Interactive Computing in Education		
Department of Technology for the Albemarle County Schools		
Maine Learning Technology Initiative		

Summary

_____

_____

_____

Statement Evaluation

Read the following statements. Then scan the article again quickly to find out if each *sentence is* **True (T), False (F),** or an **Inference (I).**

1. _____ Charlottesville Waldorf School has many computers.

2. _____ There are no computers at B.F. Yancey Elementary School.

3. _____ Some parents believe that computers can make a child smarter.

4. _____ Some studies show that students who use computers do better on standardized tests than students who do not use computers in class.

5. _____ Most public schools in the United States have computers.

6. _____ Most public school students in the United States spend a lot of time using computers in school.

7. _____ Bette Manchester believes it is sometimes difficult for teachers to use computers in class when there are not enough of them.

Read each question carefully. Either circle the letter or number of the correct answer or write your answer in the space provided.

1. Read the first paragraph of the story (lines 1–7.)

   a. Where does Jody Spanglet teach?

   _____

   b. How old are her students?
      1. 7- and 8-year-olds
      2. 12- and 13-year-olds
      3. high school age

   c. What does Jody Spanglet teach?
      1. Mathematics
      2. Science
      3. History

   d. Why is this school unusual?
      1. There are no computers.
      2. Jody Spanglet is an excellent teacher.
      3. The students enjoy their classes.

2. Read lines 8–11. How is the B.F. Yancey Elementary School different from the Charlottesville Waldorf School?

   _____

3. Read lines 15–18. An **exception** describes something that is
   a. different from the norm
   b. similar to the norm
   c. an example of the norm

4. Read lines 18–26.

   a. A **spectrum** is a

      1. computer

      2. debate

      3. range

   b. What group is at one end of the spectrum?

      _____

   c. Does this group want computers in the classrooms?

      1. Yes

      2. No

   d. What group is at the other end of the spectrum?

      _____

   e. Does this group want children to learn about computers at an early age?

      1. Yes

      2. No

   f. What group is in the middle of the spectrum?

      _____

   g. **Stand somewhere in the middle** means this group

      1. does not want computers in young children's classrooms

      2. believes young children should use computers

      3. isn't sure whether computers are good for young children

5. Read lines 44–49. Fewer students have access to computers in

   a. public schools

   b. urban schools

   c. Maine schools

6. Read lines 84–85. **Eschew** means

   a. encourage

   b. avoid

   c. support

7. Read lines 88–92.
   a. Kim McCormick is
      1. a student at the Waldorf School
      2. a parent of students at the Waldorf School
      3. an administrator at the Waldorf School
   b. Does she think her children should have computers in school?
      1. Yes
      2. No
   c. Why or why not?

   _____

8. Read lines 105–108.
   a. Why is the "mother of three children" disappointed?
      1. Her children use computers in their classrooms too much.
      2. Her children never use computers in school.
      3. The teachers do not help her children use computers in school.
   b. In these sentences, what is the teacher doing when the students are using the computers?
      1. Working at his or her desk
      2. Helping the students
      3. Assigning homework

9. Read lines 109–113. What is **one-to-one computer access**?
   a. All the students share four or five computers.
   b. Each student has his or her own laptop.
   c. The teacher works with one student at a time.

D. DICTIONARY SKILLS

Read the dictionary entry for each word and consider the context of the sentence from the passage. Write the number of the definition that is appropriate for the context on the line next to the word. Be prepared to explain your choice.

1. While the computerless Waldorf school is an exception in a nation that tends to **embrace** the technology revolution, both schools find themselves on the cutting edge of a debate about if and how computers should be introduced to children at the elementary-school level.

   embrace: _____

   > **em·brace** \im-'brās\ *vb* **em·braced;**
   > **em·brac·ing** [ME, fr. MF *embracer*, fr. OF
   > *embracier*, fr. *en-* + *brace* two arms — more
   > at BRACE] *vt* (14c) **1 a :** to clasp in the arms:
   > HUG **b :** CHERISH, LOVE **2 :** ENCIRCLE,
   > ENCLOSE **3 a :** to take up esp. readily or
   > gladly ⟨~ a cause⟩ **b :** to avail oneself of:
   > WELCOME ⟨*embraced* the opportunity to study
   > further⟩ **4 a :** to take in or include as a part,
   > item, or element of a more inclusive whole
   > ⟨charity ~s all acts that contribute to human
   > welfare⟩ **b :** to be equal or equivalent to ⟨his
   > assets *embraced* $10⟩ ~ *vi* : to participate in
   > an embrace **syn** see ADOPT, INCLUDE

2. In the fall of 2000, 98 percent of public schools had **access** to the Internet in their schools, up from 35 percent six years earlier.

   access: _____

   > **ac·cess** \'ak-,ses *also* ik-'ses\ *n* [ME, fr. MF
   > & L; MF *acces* arrival, fr. L *accessus*
   > approach, fr. *accedere* to approach—more at
   > ACCEDE] (14c) **1 a :** onset **2 b :** a fit of
   > intense feeling: OUTBURST **2 a :** permission,
   > liberty, or ability to enter, approach,
   > communicate with, or pass to and from
   > **b :** freedom or ability to obtain or make use
   > of **c :** a way or means of access **d :** the act
   > or an instance of accessing **3 :** an increase
   > by addition ⟨a sudden ~ of wealth⟩

Pronunciation Guide
\ə\abut \ə̇\ kitten, \ər\ further \a\ ash \ā\ ace \ä\ mop, mar \au̇ \ out \ch\ chin \e\ bet \ē \ easy \g\go \i\ hit \ī\ ice \j\job
\ŋ\sing \ō\ go \ȯ\ law \ȯi\ boy \th\ thin \t͟h\ the \ü\ loot \u̇\ foot \y\ yet \zh\ vision \à, k, ᴺ, œ, œ̄, ᴜᴇ, ᴜ̄ᴇ, ʸ\ *See Website below for*
Pronunciation Guide.

By permission. From *Merriam-Webster's Online Dictionary* ©2002 by Merriam-Webster, Incorporated (www.Merriam-Webster.com).

3. At one end of the **spectrum** are coalitions such as the Alliance for Childhood, which has called for a moratorium on computers for students in early childhood and elementary schools.

spectrum: _____

> **spec·trum** \\'spek-trəm\\ *n, pl* **spec·tra**
> \\-trə\\ or **spectrums** [NL, fr. L,
> appearance—more at SPECTER] (1671) **1 a :**
> a continuum of color formed when a beam of
> white light is dispersed (as by passage
> through a prism) so that its component
> wavelengths are arranged in order **b :** any
> of various continua that resemble a spectrum
> in consisting of an ordered arrangement by a
> particular characteristic (as frequency or
> energy): as (1): ELECTROMAGNETIC SPECTRUM
> (2): RADIO SPECTRUM (3): the range of
> frequencies of sound waves (4): MASS
> SPECTRUM **c :** the representation (as a plot)
> of a spectrum **2 a :** a continuous sequence
> or range ⟨a wide ~ of interests⟩ **b :** kinds of
> organisms associated with a particular
> situation (as an environment) or susceptible
> to an agent (as an antibiotic)

4. It is not as though children at Yancey are being plunked in front of a machine without interacting with teachers. But at some schools, lack of interaction is a real **concern.**

concern: _____

> **concern** *n* (1655) **1 a :** marked interest or
> regard usu. arising through a personal tie or
> relationship **b :** an uneasy state of blended
> interest, uncertainty, and apprehension
> **2 :** something that relates or belongs to one:
> AFFAIR **3 :** matter for consideration
> **4 :** an organization or establishment for
> business or manufacture **5 :** CONTRIVANCE,
> GADGET *syn* see CARE

E. *Critical Thinking Strategies*

Read each question carefully. Write your response in the space provided. Remember that there is no one correct answer. Your response depends on what **you** think.

1. The Alliance for Childhood cites "health concerns" as one reason why young students should not have computers in the classroom. What might these health concerns be?

   _____

   _____

   _____

2. Read lines 27–30. Why do these parents have a "grudging guilt" about their children?

   _____

   _____

   _____

3. Read lines 38–43. This paragraph states, "Various studies show different effects of computer use in the classroom." According to this paragraph, what factor can determine how useful computers are in the classroom?

   _____

   _____

   _____

Another Perspective

Program to Bring Laptop Computers to Rural Schools
by Melissa Nelson
Associated Press

1   Beeps from computers powering up will replace the sound of books cracking open in north-central Arkansas classrooms this fall. Free Pad computers developed by a Norwegian company are being distributed to Independence County's nearly 7,000 public school teachers and students through
5   a pilot program to put technology in rural schools. The computers will replace textbooks and library books used by kindergarten through 12th graders in the county's eight school districts.
       Independence County will be the largest test site for the program, which will include 10,300 students and teachers in Arkansas, California, Hawaii, New
10   York, Utah and Washington, D.C. Bruce Lincoln of Columbia University's Institute for Learning Technology said the program represents a changing attitude about how to meld technology and public education. "It's sharing a knowledge base with people. This has been happening in some places for a long time but not in places like Independence County," he said.
15   The New York university plans to study the Arkansas project and help with its implementation. The three-year project will cost about $14 million and will be funded through corporate, private and nonprofit sponsorships, said Sandy Morgan, founder of Kidztel, the New Hampshire company coordinating the project. Free Pads, developed by Screen Media of Oslo, Norway, weigh less than
20   two pounds and do not have hard drives. They are operated through a touch screen and include wireless Internet access. Harald Grytten, CEO of Screen

Media, said the computers were designed with children in mind. "All you have to do is point at the screen with your finger. A 9- or 10-year-old will intuitively start playing with it," he said.

25   The companies will begin installing the system in mid-June and plan a community forum later in the month to answer questions about the project. Morgan said each of the Independence County school districts have provided a list of textbooks they plan to use next year. She is working with the publishers to reproduce the books electronically. "We will have filtered Internet access in

30   the same way schools already do," she said. The Center Barnstead, N.H. mother of four said she started her electronic textbook company after noticing that her son, who had a learning disability, was drawn to the computer. "When he was on the computer or playing a video game, he was able to focus and stay on task," she said. "We have a generation of nonreaders and I became convinced that

35   schools would be the place where the electronic book market would break."

     Guy Santucci, superintendent of the 550-student Newark School District in Independence County, said several students come to his office each day asking when the computers will arrive. Santucci said the project will help link the mountainous enclaves of rural Arkansas with the rest of the world. "When kids

40   from here go to L.A., Chicago, Detroit or New York, they are at a disadvantage not just socially but globally. With a laptop they can go to all these places."

     While kids have largely embraced the project, some teachers are concerned about the changes, he said. "It can be intimidating for them, but they have to buy into the technological age," he said. "We are going to do whatever we have to do

45   to make this work because it's a $14 million project and we aren't having to pay anything." Santucci has sold the project to teachers and parents in part by telling them it could be part of the answer to school consolidation.

     Arkansas is under a state Supreme Court mandate to overhaul a public education system that the court has declared inadequate and inequitable.

50   Experts have estimated the cost of changes at $1 billion a year and some, including Gov. Mike Huckabee, have suggested finding the money through consolidating small school districts. Santucci said the technology, which includes videoconferencing, will allow school districts to share teachers in shortage subjects such as upper-level math and science. Morgan agreed. "We

55   are hoping to be one of the major solutions to the problems Arkansas educators are having," she said.

     Although the computers are composed of fragile circuitry, Santucci, Morgan and others said they aren't worried about the kids damaging the Free Pads. The computers, which cost about $450 each, are insured.

1. What is the purpose of the Free Pad computer program in north-central Arkansas?

    _____

    _____

    _____

2. Why are students of this rural area at a disadvantage without this computer project?

    _____

    _____

    _____

3. How will the technology of this program improve education in Arkansas?

    _____

    _____

    _____

G. Follow-up Activities

1. Refer to the **Self-Evaluation of Reading Strategies** on page 67. Think about the strategies you used to help yourself understand "Hop, Skip . . . and Software?" Check off the strategies you used. Think about the strategies you didn't use and try to apply them to help yourself understand the readings that follow.

2. Alone, or in pairs, interview several parents of elementary school children. Ask them whether their children use computers in school. Ask them whether they are in favor of young children using computers and ask them to explain their reasons. When you come back to class, compile your answers. Of all the parents you and your classmates interviewed, how many parents were in favor of computer use in elementary school? How many were opposed? What reasons did they have in common?

3. Work in a small group with your classmates. You are members of an elementary school committee. Your job is to set up a computer policy in your school for students in kindergarten through eighth grade. You must decide in what grade the students will begin using computers and how much time they will spend on them each day. Be prepared to explain the reasons for your decisions. When your group is finished, compare your computer policy with another group's computer policy. Are they similar or different? Now work as a class. Put all the groups' policies on the board. Work together to create a single policy for your school.

H. Topics for Discussion AND Writing

1. Choose one person whose opinion is given in the article "Hop, Skip ... and Software" and whom you agree with. Explain why you agree with this person.

2. Choose one person whose opinion is given in the article "Hop, Skip ... and Software" whom you disagree with. Explain why you disagree with this person.

3. Imagine that you are living in Virginia and you have a child who is about to start school. Which school would you prefer your child to attend: Charlottesville Waldorf School or B.F. Yancey Elementary School? Explain your answer and write your reasons for your choice.

4. **Write in your journal.** What do you think is the ideal age for a child to be introduced to computers? Why?

Chapter 1: Hop, Skip . . . and Software?

Read the passage below. Fill in the blanks with one word from the list. Use each word only once.

access	debate	enhance	loaded	particularly
advocate	devoid	exception	middle	range
age	drops	introduced	moratorium	spectrum
bonds	educators	kindle	overall	technology

While the computerless Waldorf school is an _____ (1) in a nation that tends to embrace the _____ (2) revolution, both schools find themselves on the cutting edge of a _____ (3) about if and how computers should be _____ (4) to children at the elementary-school level. At one end of the _____ (5) are coalitions such as the Alliance for Childhood, which has called for a _____ (6) on computers for students in early childhood and elementary schools. Concerns _____ (7) from health issues to the need for stronger _____ (8) between children and adults. At the other end are _____ (9) and technology enthusiasts, who believe that the use of computers at an early _____ (10) can open a child's mind to ideas and concepts that will _____ (11) a great desire for learning, and perhaps make a child "smarter." Parents and guardians stand somewhere in the _____ (12).

"I don't think an elementary school virtually _____ (13) of technology is necessarily bad," says Gene Maeroff, a professor at Columbia University's Teachers College. "Nor do I think a school _____ (14) with technology is necessarily good, or better, at meeting students' needs," he says. "Computers can _____ (15) education. But those possibilities become greater as kids get older, _____ (16) at the secondary level, and absolutely at the college or postgraduate level."

Computer technology is a fact of life in U.S. schools and homes. In the fall of 2000, 98 percent of public schools had _____ (17) to the Internet in their schools. And one in five students in public schools _____ (18) had access to a computer. In urban schools, that number _____ (19) to one in nine—which one technology _____ (20) calls "not a digital divide, but a digital chasm."

My Husband, the Outsider

Prereading Preparation

1. With two or three students, define the term *mixed marriage*. When you are finished, write your definition on the board. Compare yours with the other groups' definitions. As a class, decide what you mean by *mixed marriage*.

Your Group's Definition	The Class's Agreed-on Definition

2. Alone, think about these two questions: What is an American? When is a person an American? **Write your responses in your journal**, and think about the questions as you read the article.

3. Read the title of the article. What does Marian Hyun mean when she describes her husband as an outsider?

4. Conduct an in-class survey using the questions in the following chart. Record the responses on the chart. You will use your data later when you do an out-of-class survey on the same questions. Discuss your responses in class.

Total # of Respondents: _____ Total # of Men: _____ Total # of Women: _____

Is there a right age to get married?					
Yes		No		Not Sure	
Men	Women	Men	Women	Men	Women
%	%	%	%	%	%

Is it acceptable to marry a person of another race?					
Yes		No		Not Sure	
Men	Women	Men	Women	Men	Women
%	%	%	%	%	%

Should a son or a daughter always marry the person their parents choose?					
Yes		No		Not Sure	
Men	Women	Men	Women	Men	Women
%	%	%	%	%	%

Should a son or a daughter marry a person even if their parents disapprove of the person?					
Yes		No		Not Sure	
Men	Women	Men	Women	Men	Women
%	%	%	%	%	%

My Husband, the Outsider
by Marian Hyun
Newsday

1   When my husband-to-be and I announced our engagement, people were
curious about the kind of wedding we would have. He is an Irish-Ukrainian
from the Bronx, and a lapsed Catholic, while I am an American-born Korean
from New Jersey. Some of my husband's friends must have been expecting an
5   exotic wedding ceremony.

We disappointed many people. Far from being exotic, or even very
religious, our ceremony was performed in English by a Unitarian minister on a
hotel balcony. But when my husband and I decided to have 50 guests instead of
150, we caused an uproar among relatives and family friends, especially on the
10   Korean side.

"It's very embarrassing," my father complained. "Everyone wants to know
why you won't listen to me and invite the people you should."

"Well, whose wedding is this, anyway?" I asked.

What a dumb question. I had forgotten for a moment that I was dealing
15   with Koreans. It was bad enough that I had decided to marry a non-Korean, but
highly insulting that I wasn't giving everyone the chance to snicker over it in
person. I found out after the wedding that my father was asked, "How does it
feel to have an American son-in-law?"

"My son-in-law is a good man," he said. "Better to have a good American
20   son-in-law than a bad Korean one."

He hadn't always felt that way. For years, he ignored the non-Koreans I was
dating—it took him about a year to remember my husband's name. But when I
was a freshman in college, I dated my father's dream of a son-in-law, David, an
American-born Korean from a respected family, who was doing brilliantly at
25   Harvard and had plans for law school. When the relationship ended, my father
preferred not to acknowledge the fact.

When it became clear that David would never be his son-in-law, my father
started dropping hints at the dinner table about some handsome and delightful
young doctor working for him, who was right off the plane from Seoul—there
30   seemed to be a steady supply. This started during my senior year in college, and
continued until sometime after my engagement.

The one time I did go out with a Korean doctor was at my mother's request.
"Please, just once," she said. "One of my college friends has a son who wants to
get married, and she thought of you."

35

"You expect me to go out with a guy who lets his mommy pick his dates?" I asked.

"He's very traditional," she explained. "If you refuse to meet him, my friend will think I'm too snobby to want her son in our family. I'll lose face."

40

"OK, just this once," I said reluctantly. A few days later, I sat in an Indian restaurant with the Korean doctor. After several start-and-stop attempts at conversation, the doctor told me I should live in Korea for a while.

"Korea is a great country," he said. "I think you ought to appreciate it more. And you should learn to speak Korean. I don't understand why you can't speak your native language."

45

"English is my native language," I said. "I wish I could speak Korean, but I don't have the time to learn it now."

"You are Korean," he insisted. "You should speak your mother tongue." A mouthful of food kept me from saying more than "Mmmm," but I found myself stabbing my tandoori chicken with remarkable violence.

50

Despite our obvious incompatibility, the doctor kept asking me out. For weeks, I had to turn down invitations to dinner, movies and concerts—even rides to visit my parents—before he finally stopped calling.

During a visit to Seoul a few years later, I realized that this kind of dogged persistence during Korean courtship was quite common. In fact, my own father had used it successfully. My mother told me he proposed to her the day after

55

they were introduced at a dinner given by matchmaking friends. She told him he was crazy when she turned him down. Undaunted, he hounded her for three months until she finally gave in.

My parents have now been married for almost 40 years, but what worked for them wasn't about to work for me. I think one reason my father didn't object to having a non-Korean son-in-law—aside from actually liking my husband— was that he was relieved to have one at all.

60

When I was 24, he started asking me, "When are you going to make me a grandfather?"

65

And when I turned 25, the age when unmarried women in Korea are considered old maids, my other relatives expressed their concern.

"You better hurry up and meet someone," one of my aunts told me. "Do you have a boyfriend?"

"Yes," I said. It was 1990, and I had met my future husband a few months

70

earlier in an office where I was working as a temporary secretary.

"Is he Korean?" she asked.

"No." My aunt considered this for a moment, then said, "You better hurry up and meet someone. Do you want me to help?"

My husband saved me from spinsterhood. Just barely, in some eyes—I was

75

married at 26. We received generous gifts, many from people who hadn't been invited to the wedding. This convinced my father more than ever that we should have invited all of his friends and relatives. He felt this way for several years, until one of my sisters got engaged and made elaborate plans to feed and entertain 125 wedding guests.

80

As the expenses mounted, my father took me aside and asked me to talk to my sister.

"Tell her she should have a small, simple wedding," he said. "Like yours."

Reading Overview: Main Idea, Details, and Summary

Read the passage again. As you read, underline what you think are the most important ideas in the reading. Then, in one or two sentences, write the main idea of the reading. *Use your own words.*

Main Idea

_____

_____

_____

Details

Use the chart below to list the people the author refers to in the reading. What is each person's opinion of Marian and her marriage? Refer back to the information you underlined in the passage as a guide. When you have finished, write a brief summary of the reading. *Use your own words.*

MY HUSBAND, THE OUTSIDER

People in the reading	How does this person feel about Marian and the marriage?
Marian	

Summary

_____

_____

_____

_____

Statement Evaluation

Read the following statements. Then scan the article again quickly to find out if each sentence is **True (T), False (F),** or an **Inference (I).**

1. _____ Marian Hyun's husband is Korean.

2. _____ Marian Hyun's Korean relatives expected a very large wedding.

3. _____ Marian Hyun speaks Korean.

4. _____ Marian Hyun's parents have been married for more than 40 years.

5. _____ If a 25-year-old Korean woman is unmarried, she is an "old maid."

6. _____ Marian Hyun's father will pay for her sister's wedding.

C. Reading Analysis

Read each question carefully. Either circle the letter or number of the correct answer or write your answer in the space provided.

1. Read lines 1–5. Why were people curious about the kind of wedding Marian and her husband would have?
   a. Because they come from similar backgrounds
   b. Because they come from different backgrounds

2. Read lines 8–10. **Caused an uproar** means
   a. the family was very happy
   b. the family was very disturbed
   c. the family all disagreed

3. Read lines 17–18. What is a **son-in-law**?

   _____

4. Read lines 37–38.
   a. **Snobby** means
      1. rich
      2. superior
      3. afraid
   b. **Lose face** means
      1. hurt your face
      2. forget something
      3. become embarrassed

5. Read lines 47–49.

    a. Why was the author **stabbing my tandoori chicken with remarkable violence**?

        1. She didn't like the food.

        2. She wasn't hungry.

        3. She was angry at the Korean doctor.

    b. **Incompatibility** means that Marian and the doctor

        1. did not get along well because they didn't have anything in common

        2. got along well because they had much in common

6. Read lines 53–58.

    a. What is another expression to indicate that Marian's father showed **dogged persistence** in courting Marian's mother?

    _____

    b. These terms mean that Marian's father

        1. was shy about trying to date her mother

        2. pursued her mother insistently

        3. let her mother call him for dates

7. Read lines 80–82. Why does Marian's father ask her to tell her sister **"she should have a small, simple wedding, like yours"**?

    _____

D. DICTIONARY SKILLS

Read the dictionary entry for each word, and consider the context of the sentence from the passage. Write the number of the definition that is appropriate for the context on the line next to the word. Be prepared to explain your choice.

1. When the relationship with David ended, my father preferred not to **acknowledge** the fact.

   acknowledge: _____

---

ac·knowl·edge \ik-ˈnä-ij, ak- \ *vt* **-edged; -edg·ing** [*ac*- (as in *accord*) + *knowledge*] (15c) **1 :** to recognize the rights, authority, or status of **2 :** to disclose knowledge of or agreement with **3 a :** to express gratitude or obligation for **b :** to take notice of **c :** to make known the receipt of **4 :** to recognize as genuine or valid ⟨~ a debt⟩ *syn* ACKNOWLEDGE, ADMIT, OWN, AVOW, CONFESS mean to disclose against one's will or inclination. ACKNOWLEDGE implies the disclosing of something that has been or might be concealed ⟨*acknowledged* an earlier peccadillo⟩. ADMIT implies reluctance to disclose, grant, or concede and refers usu. to facts rather than their implications ⟨*admitted* the project was over budget⟩. OWN implies acknowledging something in close relation to oneself ⟨must *own* I know little about computers⟩. AVOW implies boldly declaring, often in the face of hostility, what one might be expected to be silent about ⟨*avowed* that he was a revolutionary⟩. CONFESS may apply to an admission of a weakness, failure, omission, or guilt ⟨*confessed* a weakness for sweets⟩.

\ə\abut \ᵊ\ kitten, \ər\ further \a\ ash \ā\ ace \ä\ mop, mar \aů \ out \ch\ chin \e\ bet \ē \ easy \g\go \i\ hit \ī\ ice \j\job \ŋ\sing \ō\ go \ȯ\ law \ȯi\ boy \th\ thin \t̲h̲\ the \ü\ loot \ů\ foot \y\ yet \zh\ vision \à, k, ⁿ, œ, œ̄, ue̱, ᵾ, ʸ\ *See Website below for* Pronunciation Guide.

2. When I was a freshman in college, I dated my father's **dream** of a son-in-law, David, an American-born Korean from a respected family, who was doing brilliantly at Harvard and had plans for law school.

dream: _____

> **dream** \'drēm \ *n, often attrib* [ME *dreem,* fr. OE *drēam* noise, joy, and ON *draumr* dream; akin to OHG *troum* dream] (13c)
> **1 :** a series of thoughts, images, or emotions occurring during sleep—compare REM SLEEP
> **2 :** an experience of waking life having the characteristics of a dream: as **a :** a visionary creation of the imagination: DAYDREAM **b :** a state of mind marked by abstraction or release from reality: REVERIE **c :** an object seen in a dreamlike state: VISION **3 :** something notable for its beauty, excellence, or enjoyable quality ⟨the new car is a ~ to operate⟩ **4 a :** a strongly desired goal or purpose ⟨a ~ of becoming president⟩ **b:** something that fully satisfies a wish: IDEAL ⟨a meal that was a gourmet's ~⟩ —
> **dream·ful** \-fəl\ *adj* — **dream·ful·ly** \-fə-lē\ *adv* — **dream·ful·ness** *n*—
> **dream·less** *adj* — **dream·less·ly** *adv* — **dream·less·ness** *n* — **dream·like** \'drēm,-līk\ *adj*

3. He is an Irish-Ukrainian from the Bronx, and a lapsed Catholic, while I am an American-born Korean from New Jersey. Some of my husband's friends must have been expecting an **exotic** wedding ceremony.

exotic: _____

> **ex·ot·ic** \ig-'zä-tik\ *adj* [L *exoticus,* fr. Gk *exōtikos,* fr. *exō*] (1599) **1 :** introduced from another country: not native to the place where found **2** *archaic :* FOREIGN, ALIEN **3 :** strikingly, excitingly, or mysteriously different or unusual **4 :** of or relating to striptease ⟨~ dancing⟩ — **ex·ot·i·cal·ly** \-ti-k(ə-)lē\ *adv* — **ex·ot·ic·ness** \-tik-nəs\ *n*

4. During dinner, the Korean doctor said, "You should learn to speak Korean. I don't understand why you can't speak your native language." "English is my native language," I said. "I wish I could speak Korean, but I don't have the time to learn it now." "You are Korean," he insisted. "You should speak your mother tongue." Despite our obvious **incompatibility,** the doctor kept asking me out.

incompatible: _____

in·com·pat·i·ble \ˌin-kəm-ˈpa-tə-bəl\ *adj* [ME, fr. MF & ML; MF, fr. ML *incompatibilis,* fr. L *in-* + ML *compatibilis* compatible] (15c) **1 :** incapable of being held by one person at one time — used of offices that make conflicting demands on the holder **2 :** not compatible: as **a :** incapable of association or harmonious coexistence ⟨~ colors⟩ **b :** unsuitable for use together because of undesirable chemical or physiological effects ⟨~ drugs⟩ **c :** not both true ⟨~ propositions⟩ **d :** incapable of blending into a stable homogeneous mixture — **incompatible** *n* — **in·com·pat·i·bly** \-blē\ *adv*

E. *Critical Thinking Strategies*

Read each question carefully. Write your response in the space provided. Remember there is no one correct answer. Your response depends on what **you** think.

1. Read the first paragraph. Why do you think Marian's husband's family were expecting an exotic wedding ceremony?

    _____

    _____

2. What qualities do you think Marian's father looked for in a possible husband for his daughter?

    _____

    _____

3. What did Marian's mother mean by "losing face"?

    _____

    _____

4. What can you infer about Marian's attitude when she said to her mother, "You expect me to go out with a guy who lets his mommy pick his dates"?

    _____

    _____

5. Reading between the lines, what was Marian's aunt actually saying when she repeated, "You better hurry up and meet someone"?

    _____

    _____

6. Marian talks about her opinion and describes how her mother and father feel. However, she does not discuss her husband's point of view. Why do you think she decided not to write about his opinion?

_____

_____

7. What was the author's tone? For example, was she humorous, serious, sarcastic, etc.? What was it that makes you think so?

_____

_____

Another Perspective

Unwelcome In Chinatown

She Looks the Part, But She Doesn't Speak the Language
by Amy Wu
The New York Times

1   When I go to Chinatown for breakfast with my parents or my relatives from Hong Kong, we are ushered to the best table, offered a variety of special dishes and treated to warm smiles and solicitous service by the dim sum ladies.

      You might think that because I am Chinese—with the standard straight
5   hair, yellow skin and slanted eyes—I would have an inside track in Chinatown. But there are hundreds of men and women like me in New York who actually get short shrift there because we're ABCs, American-born Chinese, and we don't speak Cantonese.

      Whether it's an outdoor market, a stationery store, a bakery or a restaurant,
10   the routine is always the same. ABCs are initially greeted with a smile and a friendly word in Cantonese. Then, when it's discovered that we don't understand, the word, smile, and any pretense of friendliness disappear.

It can be embarrassing. One time, a dim sum lady asked me something after she had chatted with my father. "She doesn't speak Cantonese," my father said. The woman turned scarlet. "What, you never taught her?!" she asked indignantly.

Actually, when I was little, my parents enrolled me in a Saturday morning private school to learn Chinese language and culture. I dropped out when I was 7, after a year or two. I had better things to do on a weekend—mainly to play with my American friends. I wanted nothing more than to be like them, and that's what I became. Now, in Chinatown, I pay the price.

Tourists get better treatment than ABCs. Ladies in cheepows bow to them. Waiters fill teapots without being asked. Managers make polite chit-chat, asking how they like Chinatown. Tourists have an excuse for not knowing Cantonese.

Well, nobody asked, but I love Chinatown—the smells of fried noodles, the hurly-burly, the feeling of being in another world that is like a little piece of my heritage. I don't think I deserve the treatment I receive there.

A Chinatown friend says I should be more understanding. "They live in tiny rooms, in poverty," she said. "They have very little to be proud about except this language no one else understands. You're either in or out."

To them, I'm just another Americanized young person, a failure, a traitor. Sure I understand, but most of the time I'm just plain angry. It's not that I want to be accepted, just respected.

Whenever my downtown ABC friends and I want Chinese food without the insults, we go to a take-out place near our New York University dorm. The lo mein is dry and the vegetables are watery, but the cook gives us extra fortune cookies and orange slices and jokes with us in English. He makes us feel at home. Of course, he is an ABC, too.

1. Why does Amy Wu feel unwelcome in Chinatown?

    _____

    _____

2. Do you think Amy Wu's experience as an American-born Chinese is a typical experience? Explain your answer.

    _____

    _____

    _____

3. Compare Marian Hyun's experience with that of Amy Wu's. How do you think their upbringing might have been similar? How might it have been different?

    _____

    _____

    _____

4. Apparently, neither Marian's parents nor Amy's parents raised their daughters to be bilingual. Why do you think this was so? What do you think about the consequences of Marian and Amy being monolingual? About being so "Americanized"?

    _____

    _____

    _____

Follow-up Activities

1. Refer to the **Self-Evaluation of Reading Strategies** on page 67. Think about the strategies you used to help yourself understand "My Husband, the Outsider." Check off the strategies you used. Think about the strategies you didn't use, and try to apply them to help yourself understand the readings that follow.

2. Alone, or in pairs, interview several people. Use the chart below. When you return to class, compile your data, using the chart on the next page.

MARRIAGE/NATIONALITY SURVEY

The purpose of this questionnaire is to collect data regarding people's opinions about marriage.

Questions	#1	#2	#3	#4
a. Interviewee is Male/Female (circle one)	M/F	M/F	M/F	M/F
b. Interviewee's age. Are you: under 20? 20–30? 30–40? 40–45? 50+?				
c. What nationality are you?				
1. Is there a "right" age to get married?				
2. If you answered "Yes" to #1, is the right age the same for men and women?				
3. Is it acceptable for someone to marry a person of another race?				
4. Should a son or a daughter always marry the person their parents choose?				
5. Should a son or a daughter marry a person even if their parents disapprove of the person?				
6. What is an American?				
#1.				
#2.				
#3.				
#4.				

DATA COMPILATION SHEET

Total # of Respondents: _____

Total # of Men: _____ Total # of Women: _____

Is there a "right" age to get married?

Yes		No		Not Sure	
Men	Women	Men	Women	Men	Women
%	%	%	%	%	%

Is it acceptable to marry a person of another race?

Yes		No		Not Sure	
Men	Women	Men	Women	Men	Women
%	%	%	%	%	%

Should a son or a daughter always marry the person their parents choose?

Yes		No		Not Sure	
Men	Women	Men	Women	Men	Women
%	%	%	%	%	%

Should a son or a daughter marry a person even if their parents disapprove of the person?

Yes		No		Not Sure	
Men	Women	Men	Women	Men	Women
%	%	%	%	%	%

3. a. Refer to your data. What percent of people would probably approve of Marian's decision to marry a non-Korean? Was there a difference in the responses of men and women? If so, what were the differences? Why do you think men and women responded differently?

   b. What are the similarities and differences between your responses as a class and your interviewees' responses? When *is* a person an American? What *is* an American?

4. The following chart shows the percentage of people of various races who got married in the United States **and** who married a person of another race. These statistics cover the years 1970 to 1993. Look at it carefully, then answer the questions that follow.

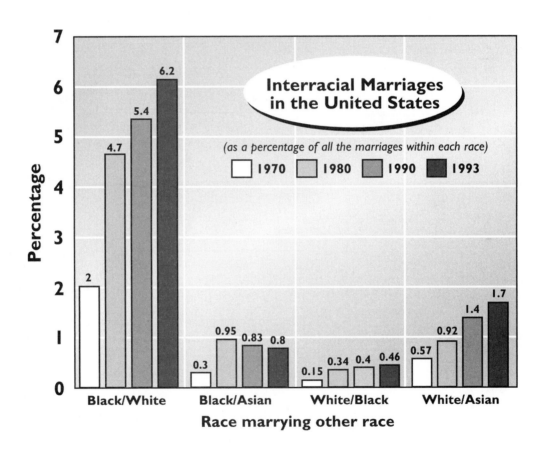

a. Which race has the highest percentage of interracial marriages?

_____

b. Which rate is higher, the percent of black marriages that involve whites or the percent of white marriages that involve blacks?

_____

c. Which race has the lowest percentage of interracial marriages?

_____

H. *Topics for Discussion* AND *Writing*

1. Think about the people in the article "My Husband, the Outsider": Marian, her father, her mother, her dates, her husband. Marian describes how she feels and gives us an idea about how her mother and father feel. How do you think her dates felt? How do you think her husband feels about his new in-laws? How do you think Marian's husband's parents might feel about his marriage?

2. Discuss the conflicts that Marian Hyun had with her family and with her dates. What were some of the causes of these conflicts? For example, were they parent–child disagreements? Were they the result of cultural differences?

3. From this chapter, we know that Marian does not speak Korean and Amy does not speak Cantonese. Why didn't they learn these languages? Do you think they should be able to speak them? Explain your answer.

4. By yourself, think about your initial answers to these two questions: When is a person an American? What is an American? Do you think any differently after reading the two articles in this chapter? Then, in small groups, discuss your responses. Do you have similar ideas about when a person is an American? About what an American is?

5. **Write in your journal.** Marian did not follow her parents' wish that she marry a Korean man. What is your opinion about her decision?

Cloze Quiz

Chapter 2: My Husband the Outsider

Read the passage below. Fill in the blanks with one word from the list. Use each word only once.

acknowledge	exotic	incompatibility	once	remember
curious	gave in	lose face	persistence	snobby
disappointed	hounded	object	preferred	uproar
embarrassing	ignored	old maids	reluctantly	violence

When my husband-to-be and I announced our engagement, people were _____ about the kind of wedding we would have. He is an (1) Irish-Ukrainian from the Bronx, and a lapsed Catholic, while I am an American-born Korean from New Jersey. Some of my husband's friends must have been expecting an _____ wedding ceremony. (2)

We _____ many people. Far from being exotic, or even very (3) religious, our ceremony was performed in English by a Unitarian minister on a hotel balcony. But when my husband and I decided to have 50 guests instead of 150, we caused an _____ among relatives and family (4) friends, especially on the Korean side.

"It's very _____," my father complained. "Everyone wants to (5) know why you won't listen to me and invite the people you should."

"Well, whose wedding is this, anyway?" I asked.

What a dumb question. I had forgotten for a moment that I was dealing with Koreans. It was bad enough that I had decided to marry a non-Korean, but highly insulting that I wasn't giving everyone the chance to snicker over it in person. I found out after the wedding that my father was asked, "How does it feel to have an American son-in-law?"

"My son-in-law is a good man," he said. "Better to have a good American son-in-law than a bad Korean one."

He hadn't always felt that way. For years, he _____ the (6) non-Koreans I was dating—it took him about a year to _____ my (7) husband's name. But when I was a freshman in college, I dated my father's dream of a son-in-law, David, an American-born Korean from a respected family, who was doing brilliantly at Harvard and had plans for law school.

When the relationship ended, my father _____ not to (8) _____ the fact. (9)

The one time I did go out with a Korean doctor was at my mother's request. "Please, just _____," she said. "One of my college friends (10) has a son who wants to get married, and she thought of you."

"You expect me to go out with a guy who lets his mommy pick his dates?" I asked.

"He's very traditional," she explained. "If you refuse to meet him, my friend will think I'm too _____ to want her son in our family. I'll (11) _____." (12)

"OK, just this once," I said _____. A few days later, I sat in an (13) Indian restaurant with the Korean doctor. After several start-and-stop attempts at conversation, the doctor told me I should live in Korea for a while.

"Korea is a great country," he said. "I think you ought to appreciate it more. And you should learn to speak Korean. I don't understand why you can't speak your native language."

"English is my native language," I said. "I wish I could speak Korean, but I don't have the time to learn it now."

"You are Korean," he insisted. "You should speak your mother tongue." A mouthful of food kept me from saying more than "Mmmm," but I found myself stabbing my tandoori chicken with remarkable _____.
(14)

Despite our obvious _____, the doctor kept asking me out.
(15)
For weeks, I had to turn down invitations to dinner, movies and concerts—even rides to visit my parents—before he finally stopped calling.

During a visit to Seoul a few years later, I realized that this kind of dogged _____ during Korean courtship was quite common. In fact, my
(16)
own father had used it successfully. My mother told me he proposed to her the day after they were introduced at a dinner given by matchmaking friends. She told him he was crazy when she turned him down. Undaunted, he _____ her for three months until she finally _____.
(17)   (18)

My parents have now been married for almost 40 years, but what worked for them wasn't about to work for me. I think one reason my father didn't _____ to having a non-Korean son-in-law—aside from actually
(19)
liking my husband—was that he was relieved to have one at all.

When I was 24, he started asking me, "When are you going to make me a grandfather?"

And when I turned 25, the age when unmarried women in Korea are considered _____, my other relatives expressed their concern.
(20)

"You better hurry up and meet someone," one of my aunts told me. "Do you have a boyfriend?"

"Yes," I said. It was 1990, and I had met my future husband a few months earlier in an office where I was working as a temporary secretary.

"Is he Korean?" she asked.

"No." My aunt considered this for a moment, then said, "You better hurry up and meet someone. Do you want me to help?"

CHAPTER

3

Beyond Rivalry

Prereading Preparation

Work in your groups to discuss the following questions.

1. How did you get along with your brothers and sisters when you were children? Which sibling did you get along with the best?

2. What kind of relationship do you have now with your brothers and sisters?

3. What do you think happens to the relationship between siblings as they get older? Do they feel closer to each other? Why do you think so?

4. Of the following pairs of siblings, which pair do you think is usually the closest for most people? Why do you think so?

   a.   A brother and a sister
   b.   Two sisters
   c.   Two brothers

5. Read the title of this article. What aspect of the sibling relationship do you think the writer will focus on?

6. Do an in-class survey of the questions you discussed. When you are finished, compile your data. You will use this information later to compare your responses with the responses of the people you will interview outside the class.

SIBLING SURVEY

Questions	#1	#2	#3	#4
1. How many brothers and sisters do you have?				
2. Where are you in terms of birth order (the oldest, the middle child, the youngest)?				
3. As a child, how well did you get along with your siblings? very well OK not very well badly				
4. Which sibling did you get along with the best?				
5. How do you get along with your siblings today? very well OK not very well badly				
6. Of the following pairs of siblings, which pair do you think is usually the closest? a. a brother and a sister b. two sisters c. two brothers				
7. Which person in your family usually takes responsibility for getting family members together?				

Beyond Rivalry

by Elizabeth Stark
Psychology Today

1   During childhood, sisters and brothers are a major part of each other's lives, for better or for worse. As adults they may drift apart as they become involved in their own careers, marriages and families. But in later life, with retirement, an empty nest, and parents and sometimes spouses gone, brothers and sisters often
5   turn back to each other for a special affinity and link to the past.
   "In the stressful, fast-paced world we live in, the sibling relationship becomes for many the only intimate connection that seems to last," says psychologist Michael Kahn of the University of Hartford. Friends and neighbors may move away, former coworkers are forgotten, marriages break up, but no
10   matter what, our sisters and brothers remain our sisters and brothers.

This late-life bond may be especially important to the "Baby Boom" generation[1] now in adulthood, who average about two or three siblings apiece. High divorce rates and the decision by many couples to have only one or no children will force members of this generation to look to their brothers and sisters for support in old age. And, as psychologist Deborah Gold of the Duke Center for the Study of Aging and Human Development points out, "Since people are living longer and are healthier longer, they will be more capable of giving help."

Critical events can bring siblings together or deepen an existing rift, according to a study by psychologists Helgola Ross and Joel Milgram of the University of Cincinnati. Parental sickness or death is a prime example. Ross and Milgram found that siblings immersed in rivalry and conflict were even more torn apart by the death or sickness of a parent. Those siblings who had been close since childhood became closer.

In a study of older people with sisters and brothers, Gold found that about 20 percent said they were either hostile or indifferent toward their siblings. Reasons for the rifts ranged from inheritance disputes to animosity between spouses. But many of those who had poor relationships felt guilt and remorse. A man who hadn't spoken with his sister in 20 years described their estrangement as a "festering sore."

Although most people in Ross and Milgram's study admitted to some lingering rivalry, it was rarely strong enough to end the relationship. Only 4 out of the 55 people they interviewed had completely broken with their siblings and only 1 of the 4 felt comfortable with the break, leaving the researchers to ask, "Is it psychologically impossible to disassociate oneself from one's siblings in the way one can forget old friends or even former mates?"

As brothers and sisters advance into old age, "closeness increases and rivalry diminishes," explains Victor Cicirelli, a psychologist at Purdue University. Most of the elderly people he interviewed said they had supportive and friendly dealings and got along well or very well with their brothers and sisters. Only 4 percent got along poorly.

Gold found that as people age they often become more involved with and interested in their siblings. Fifty-three percent of those she interviewed said that contact with their sisters and brothers increased in late adulthood. With family and career obligations reduced, many said they had more time for each other. Others said that they felt it was "time to heal wounds." A man who had recently reconciled with his brother told Gold, "There's something that lets older people put aside the bad deeds of the past and focus a little on what we need now . . . especially when it's brothers and sisters."

[1]"Baby Boom" generation refers to the people who were born in the United States from 1946 to 1964, when the birth rate increased dramatically. Seventeen million children were born during this 18-year period.

Another reason for increased contact was anxiety about a sister's or brother's declining health. Many would call more often to "check in" and see how the other was doing. Men especially reported feeling increased responsibility for a sibling; women were more likely to cite emotional motivations such as feelings of empathy and security.

Siblings also assume special importance as other sources of contact and support dwindle. Each of us moves through life with a "convoy" of people who supply comfort and nurturance, says psychologist Toni C. Antonucci of the University of Michigan. As we age, the size of the convoy gradually declines because of death, sickness or moving. "Brothers and sisters who may not have been important convoy members earlier in life can become so in old age," Gold says. And they do more than fill in gaps. Many people told Gold that the loneliness they felt could not be satisfied by just anyone. They wanted a specific type of relationship, one that only someone who had shared their past could provide.

This far-reaching link to the past is a powerful bond between siblings in later life. "There's a review process we all go through in old age to resolve whether we are pleased with our lives," Gold explains. "A sibling can help retrieve a memory and validate our experiences. People have said to me, 'I can remember some with my spouse or with friends. But the only person who goes all the way back is my sister or brother.'"

Cicirelli agrees that reviewing the past together is a rewarding activity. "Siblings have a very important role in maintaining a connection to early life," he says. "Discussing the past evokes the warmth of early family life. It validates and clarifies events of the early years." Furthermore, he has found that encouraging depressed older people to reminisce with a sister or brother can improve their morale.

Some of the factors that affect how much contact siblings will have, such as how near they live, are obvious. Others are more unexpected—for example, whether there is a sister in the clan. Cicirelli found that elderly people most often feel closest to a sister and are more likely to keep in touch through her. According to Gold, sisters, by tradition, often assume a caretaking and kin-keeping role, especially after the death of their mother. "In many situations you see two brothers who don't talk to each other that much but keep track of each other through their sisters," she says. Researchers have found that the bond between sisters is strongest, followed by the one between sisters and brothers and, last, between brothers.

Sisters and brothers who live near each other will, as a matter of course, see more of each other. But Cicirelli says that proximity is not crucial to a strong relationship later in life. "Because of multiple chronic illnesses, people in their

80s and 90s can't get together that easily. Even so, the sibling seems to evoke positive feelings based on the images or feelings inside."

Gold's findings support this assertion. During a two-year period, contact among her respondents decreased slightly, but positive feelings increased. "Just the idea that the sibling is alive, that 'there is someone I can call,' is comforting."

Although older people may find solace in the thought that their siblings are there if they need them, rarely do they call each other for help or offer each other instrumental support, such as loaning money, running errands or performing favors. "Even though you find siblings saying that they'd be glad to help each other and saying they would ask for help if necessary, rarely do they ask," Cicirelli points out.

Gold believes that there are several reasons siblings don't turn to each other more for instrumental help. First, since they are usually about the same age, they may be equally needy or frail. Another reason is that many people consider their siblings safety nets who will save them after everything else has failed. A son or daughter will almost always be turned to first. It's more acceptable in our society to look up or down the family ladder for help than sideways.

Finally, siblings may not turn to each other for help because of latent rivalry. They may believe that if they need to call on a brother or sister they are admitting that the other person is a success and "I am a failure." Almost all of the people in Gold's study said they would rather continue on their own than ask their sister or brother for help. But she found that a crisis beyond control would inspire "a 'rallying' of some or all siblings around the brother or sister in need."

Despite the quarreling and competition many people associate with the mere mention of their sisters and brothers, most of us, Gold says, will find "unexpected strengths in this relationship in later life."

A. Reading Overview: Main Idea, Details, and Summary

Read the passage again. As you read, underline what you think are the most important ideas in the reading. Then, in one or two sentences, write the main idea of the reading. *Use your own words.*

Main Idea

_____

_____

_____

Details

Use the outline below to organize the information about siblings'
relationships. Refer back to the information you underlined in the passage as
a guide. When you have finished, write a brief summary of the reading. *Use
your own words.*

BEYOND RIVALRY

I.   Social Connections

    A.

        1. have careers

        2.

        3.

    B. Older Adult Siblings

        1.

        2.

        3.

II. Effects of Critical Events in Siblings' Lives

    A.

    B.

III.

    A.

    B.

    C. 53 percent increased contact

        1.

        2. anxiety about sibling's health

        3.

        4. need link to the past

IV.

    A. proximity

    B.

V. Factors Affecting Why Siblings Don't Ask Each Other for Help

    A.

    B.

    C.

Summary

_____

_____

_____

_____

Statement Evaluation

Read the following statements. Then scan the article again quickly to find out if each sentence is **True (T), False (F),** or **Not Mentioned (NM)** in the article.

1. _____ Critical events always bring siblings closer together.

2. _____ Most older people are angry or hostile towards their siblings.

3. _____ Many brothers and sisters have more contact with each other as they age.

4. _____ Older male siblings argue more than older female siblings do.

5. _____ Older brothers and sisters enjoy talking together about the past.

6. _____ The age difference between siblings is an important factor in sibling rivalry.

7. _____ Older people prefer to call their siblings for help instead of their children.

Read each question carefully. Either circle the letter or number of the correct answer or write your answer in the space provided.

1. Read Lines 19–24.
   a. **"Critical events can bring siblings together or deepen an existing rift."** This sentence means that critical events
      1. can have opposite effects on siblings
      2. always make siblings feel closer
      3. always pull siblings apart
   b. What are examples of **critical events** in the paragraph?

   _____

2. Read lines 29–30.
   a. What is an **estrangement**?
      1. A family
      2. A closeness
      3. A separation
   b. How do you know?

   _____

3. Read lines 31–36. Why did the researchers ask this question?
   a. The majority of the people in the study did not have contact with their siblings. Researchers wonder why.
   b. The majority of the people in the study had contact with their siblings. Researchers wonder why.

4. Read lines 37–39. The authors state that "closeness increases and rivalry diminishes." **Diminishes** is
   a. a synonym of **increases**
   b. an antonym of **increases**

5. Read lines 55–61.

    a. Which word in this paragraph is a synonym of **dwindle**?

    _____

    b. What is a **convoy** of people?

    _____

    c. **"Brothers and sisters who may not have been important convoy members earlier in life can become so in old age."** In this sentence, **so** means

        1. siblings can become important convoy members
        2. as a result
        3. very

6. Read lines 69–70. What is the meaning of **all the way back**?

    _____

7. Read lines 77–82.

    a. What is the meaning of **clan**?

        1. Family
        2. Old people
        3. Hospital

    b. What is the meaning of **kin**?

        1. Health
        2. Communication
        3. Relatives

8. Read lines 87–91. What word in this paragraph is a synonym of the phrase **live near each other**?

    _____

9. Read lines 95–98.

    a. What does **solace** mean?

        1. Sibling
        2. Comfort
        3. Anger

    b. What are examples of **instrumental support**?

    _____

    c. How do you know?

    _____

D. DICTIONARY SKILLS

Read the entry for each word, and consider the context of the sentence from the passage. Write the number of the definition that is appropriate for the context on the line next to the word. Be prepared to explain your choice.

1. The late-life **bond** between brothers and sisters may be especially important to the "Baby Boom" generation now in adulthood.

    Brothers and sisters who may not have been important convoy members earlier in life can become so in old age. Many people said that the loneliness they felt could not be satisfied by just anyone. They wanted a specific type of relationship, one that only someone who had shared their past could provide. This far-reaching link to the past is a powerful **bond** between siblings in later life.

    bond: _____

> **bond** \\'bänd\\ *n* [ME, *band, bond*—more at
> BAND] (12c) **1 :** something that binds or
> restrains : FETTER **2 :** a binding agreement :
> COVENANT **3 a :** a band or cord used to tie
> something **b :** a material or device for
> binding **c :** an attractive force that holds
> together the atoms, ions, or groups of atoms
> in a molecule or crystal **d :** an adhesive,
> cementing material, or fusible ingredient that
> combines, unites, or strengthens **4 :** a
> uniting or binding element or force : TIE ⟨the
> ~*s* of friendship⟩ **5 a :** an obligation made
> binding by a money forfeit; *also* : the amount
> of the money guarantee **b :** one who acts as
> bail or surety **c :** an interest-bearing
> certificate of public or private indebtedness
> **d :** an insurance agreement pledging surety
> for financial loss caused to another by the act
> or default of a third person or by some
> contingency over which the third person may
> have no control **6 :** the systematic lapping
> of brick in a wall **7 :** the state of goods
> made, stored, or transported under the care of
> bonded agencies until the duties or taxes on
> them are paid **8 :** a 100-proof straight
> whiskey aged at least four years under
> government supervision before being bottled
> — called also *bonded whiskey*
> **9 :** BOND PAPER

\ə\abut \ᵊ\ kitten, \ər\ further \a\ ash \ā\ ace \ä\ mop, mar \au̇\ out \ch\ chin \e\ bet \ē \ easy \g\go \i\ hit \ī\ ice \j\job \ŋ\sing \ō\ go \ȯ\ law \ȯi\ boy \th\ thin \t͟h\ the \ü\ loot \u̇\ foot \y\ yet \zh\ vision \à, k̲, ⁿ, œ, œ̄, ᵫ, ᵫ̄, ʸ\ *See Website below for* Pronunciation Guide.

By permission. From *Merriam-Webster's Online Dictionary* ©2002 by Merriam-Webster, Incorporated (www.Merriam-Webster.com).

2. A sibling can help retrieve a memory and validate our experiences. Discussing the past can **evoke** the warmth of early family life.

    Because of multiple chronic illnesses, people in their 80s and 90s can't get together that easily. Even so, the sibling seems to **evoke** positive feelings based on the images or feelings inside.

    evoke: _____

> **evoke** \i'vōk\ *vt* **evoked; evok·ing** [F *évoquer,* fr. L *evocare,* fr. *e-* + *vocare* to call — more at VOCATION] (ca. 1626) **1 :** to call forth or up: as **a :** CONJURE 2a ⟨~ evil spirits⟩ **b :** to cite esp. with approval or for support : INVOKE **c :** to bring to mind or recollection ⟨this place ~*s* memories⟩ **2 :** to recreate imaginatively *syn* see EDUCE

3. The sibling relationship becomes for many the only intimate connection that seems to **last.** Friends and neighbors may move away, former coworkers are forgotten, marriages break up, but our brothers and sisters remain our brothers and sisters.

    last: _____

> **last** \'last\ *vb* [ME, fr. OER *lǣstan* to last, follow; akin to OE *lāst* footprint] *vi* (bef. 12c) **1 :** to continue in time **2 a :** to remain fresh or unimpaired : ENDURE **b :** to manage to continue (as in a course of action) **c :** to continue to live ~ *vt* **1 :** to continue in existence or action as long as or longer than — often used with *out* ⟨couldn't ~ out the training program⟩ **2:** to be enough for the needs of ⟨the supplies will ~ them a week⟩ *syn* see CONTINUE—**last·er** *n*

4. A sibling can help retrieve a memory and **validate** our experiences. Siblings have a very important role in maintaining a connection to early life. Discussing the past evokes the warmth of early family life. It **validates** and clarifies events of the early years.

   validate: _____

---

val·i·date \'va-lə-ˌdāt\ *vt* **-dat·ed; -dat·ing** (1648) **1 a :** to make legally valid **b :** to grant official sanction to by marking **c :** to confirm the validity of (an election); *also :* to declare (a person) elected **2 :** to support or corroborate on a sound or authoritative basis ⟨experiments designed to ~ the hypothesis⟩ *syn* see CONFIRM

E. Critical Thinking Strategies

Read each question carefully. Write your response in the space provided. Remember that there is no one correct answer. Your response depends on what **you** think.

1. Why might the "Baby Boom" generation have a high divorce rate? Why might this group have fewer children than previous American generations?

   _____

   _____

   _____

2. Is there a difference between men's and women's feelings toward their siblings? Explain your answer.

   _____

   _____

   _____

3. Why do sisters often assume a caretaking role, especially after the death of their mother?

   _____

   _____

   _____

4. Why did contact among siblings decrease, while positive feelings among them increased?

   _____

   _____

   _____

Another Perspective

Middle Children and Their Position in the Family

by Dr. Kevin Leman

(excerpt from *Living in a Step-Family without Getting Stepped On*)

1   Middle-born children will tell you that they usually didn't feel all that special while growing up. The first-born had his spot—carrier of the family banner and responsible for everything. The last born had his comfy little role, but the middle born had no distinctive place to call his own. . . .

5   Middle-borns just seem to be easily overlooked, and maybe that's why there are so few pictures of them in the family photo album. There may be hundreds, seemingly thousands, of pictures of the firstborn. And the baby of the family will make sure she attracts enough attention to fill a few album pages. For some strange reason, however, which I have confirmed by polling middle-born

10   children around the world, there are seldom many pictures of the middle child, and what photos there are have him included with the others—squeezed again between the older sibling and the younger sibling.

Another thing that can be said of many middle-born children is that they typically place great importance on their peer group. The middle child is well known for going outside the home to make friends faster than anybody else in the family. When a child feels like a fifth wheel at home, friends become very important; as a result, many middle children (but not all, of course) tend to be the social lions of the family. While firstborns, typically, have fewer friends, middle children often have many.

Middle children have a propensity to leave home first and live farther away from the family than anyone else. I observed a dramatic illustration of this tendency while I was a guest on Oprah Winfrey's show. The subject that day was sibling rivalry. Three charming young women, all sisters, were among the guests, and we quickly learned that the firstborn and the last born were residents of the Eastern state where they had grown up. They had settled down near their parents and other family members. But the middle child had moved to the West Coast.

I suppose she could have gotten another two thousand miles farther away by moving to Hawaii, but her point was still well made. Middle children are the ones who will most often physically distance themselves from the rest of the family. It's not necessarily because they're on the outs with everyone else. They simply like to do their own thing, make their own friends, and live their own lives. . . .

All of this is not to say that middle children totally ignore their siblings or the rest of the family. One common characteristic of the middle child is that she is a good mediator or negotiator. She comes naturally into this role because she's often right in the middle, between big brother and little sister, whatever the case may be. And because she can't have Mom or Dad all to herself, she learns the fine art of compromise. Obviously, these skills are assets in adult life, and middle children often become the best adjusted adults in the family.

Questions for "Middle Children and Their Position in the Family"

1. List some of the personality traits and behaviors that Dr. Leman attributes to middle children.

   _____

   _____

   _____

2. How do you think these traits and behaviors might affect the middle child's relationship with his/her siblings during childhood?

   _____

   _____

   _____

3. How do you think these traits and behaviors might affect the middle child's relationship with his/her siblings later on in life?

   _____

   _____

   _____

G. Follow-up Activities

1. Refer to the **Self-Evaluation of Reading Strategies** on the next page. Think about the strategies you used to help yourself understand "Beyond Rivalry." Check off the strategies you used. Evaluate your strategy use over the first three chapters. Which strategies have you begun to use that you didn't use in the first or second chapter? Which strategies do you use consistently? Which additional strategies do you use that you have added to the list? To what extent have you applied these strategies to other reading you do?

SELF-EVALUATION OF READING STRATEGIES

Strategies	"Hop, Skip … and Software"	"My Husband, the Outsider"	"Beyond Rivalry"
I read the title and try to predict what the reading will be about.			
I use my knowledge of the world to help me understand the text.			
I read as though I *expect* the text to have meaning.			
I use illustrations to help me understand the text.			
I ask myself questions about the text.			
I use a variety of types of context clues.			
I take chances in order to identify meaning.			
I continue if I am not successful.			
I identify and underline main ideas.			
I connect details with main ideas.			
I summarize the reading in my own words.			
I skip unnecessary words.			
I look up words correctly in the dictionary.			
I connect the reading to other material I have read.			
I do not translate into my native language.			

2. Alone, or in pairs, interview several people outside class. When you return to class, compile your data. What are the similarities and differences between your responses as a class and your interviewees' responses?

SIBLING SURVEY

The purpose of this questionnaire is to collect data regarding people and their siblings. Interview people with at least one sibling.

	#1	#2	#3	#4
Interviewee's gender	M/F	M/F	M/F	M/F
Questions				
1. How many brothers and sisters do you have?				
2. Where are you in terms of birth order (oldest, middle child, youngest)?				
3. As a child, how well did you get along with your siblings? very well OK not very well badly				
4. Which sibling did you get along with the best?				
5. How do you get along with your siblings today? very well OK not very well badly				
6. Of the following pairs of siblings, which pair do you think is usually the closest? a. A brother and a sister b. Two sisters c. Two brothers				
7. Which person in your family usually takes responsibility for getting family members together?				

H. Topics for Discussion AND Writing

1. Write a composition about one of your siblings. What was your relationship like? Why did you feel this way about each other? How is your relationship today? If you are an only child, write about whether you would have preferred to have siblings. Explain your preference.

2. Do you think it is important for children to have brothers and sisters? If so, how many? Do you think that only children may be at a disadvantage when they get older? Why or why not? Discuss this issue with your classmates.

3. In your opinion, how important is the bond between siblings? How does this bond change as siblings get older? Give examples from your own life. When you need help, who do you turn to? Why?

4. What is your birth order? Do you think your role in your family has been influenced by your position? If so, in what ways? Write a composition.

5. **Write in your journal.** Which member of your family assumes the kin-keeping role described in this article? Why?

Chapter 3: Beyond Rivalry

Read the passage below. Fill in the blanks with one word from the list. Use each word only once.

close	events	last	old age	rift
divorce	example	link	parent	sibling
drift	generation	marriages	relationships	spouses
estrangement	hostile	neighbors	retirement	worse

During childhood, sisters and brothers are a major part of each other's lives, for better or for _____. As adults they may
(1)

_____ apart as they become involved in their own careers,
(2)

marriages and families. But in later life, with _____, an empty
(3)

nest, and parents and sometimes _____ gone, brothers and
(4)

sisters often turn back to each other for a special affinity and

_____ to the past.
(5)

"In the stressful, fast-paced world we live in, the _____
(6)

relationship becomes for many the only intimate connection that seems to

_____," says psychologist Michael Kahn of the University of
(7)

Hartford. Friends and _____ may move away, former coworkers
(8)

are forgotten, _____ break up, but no matter what, our sisters
(9)

and brothers remain our sisters and brothers.

This late-life bond may be especially important to the "Baby Boom"

_____ now in adulthood, who average about two or three
(10)

siblings apiece. High _____ rates and the decision by many
(11)

couples to have only one or no children will force members of this generation to look to their brothers and sisters for support in _____.
(12)

Critical _____ can bring siblings together or deepen an
(13)
existing _____. Parental sickness or death is a prime
(14)
_____. Ross and Milgram found that siblings immersed in rivalry
(15)
and conflict were even more torn apart by the death or sickness of a
_____. Those siblings who had been _____ since
(16)   (17)
childhood became closer.

In a study of older people with sisters and brothers, Gold found that
about 20 percent said they were either _____ or indifferent
(18)
toward their siblings. Reasons for the rifts ranged from inheritance disputes
to animosity between spouses. But many of those who had poor
_____ felt guilt and remorse. A man who hadn't spoken with his
(19)
sister in 20 years described their _____ as a "festering sore."
(20)

Unit 1 Review

J. Crossword Puzzle

Read the clues on the next page. Write the answers in the correct spaces in the puzzle.

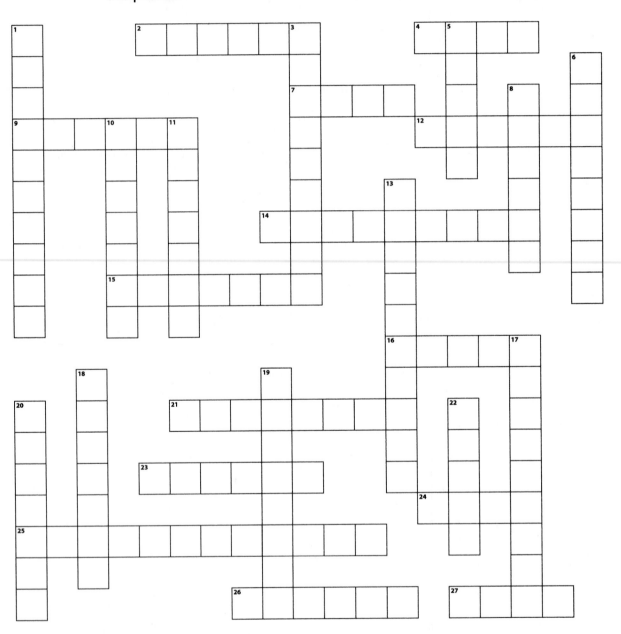

Crossword Puzzle Clues

Across

2. We offer _____ to someone when we try to comfort him.
4. A break
7. A suit or action in law
9. When I have _____ to the Internet, I can go online whenever I wish.
12. When we _____ with others, we take opposite sides on an issue.
14. Able to speak two languages
15. Apprehension or worry
16. Bring to mind; call forth a memory
21. Confirm; verify
23. Unusual; excitingly different
24. Endure; remain unimpaired
25. Unable to get along with because of differences
26. Option
27. A tie; a uniting force

Down

1. Estrangement
3. An _____ is something that is different from the norm.
5. "Read between the lines"
6. Range
8. Clan
10. Take up readily or gladly
11. Brother or sister
13. Promise or commitment to marry
17. Children go to school to get an _____.
18. Improve
19. Dwindle; decrease
20. Marriage ceremony
22. My _____ job is a dream job.

1. There are not enough qualified people in the United States to fill all the high-technology job openings in the country. What do you think are the main reasons for this job shortage?

2. Read the statements below and then watch the video once or twice. Decide whether each sentence is **True (T), False (F),** or an **Inference (I).**

   A. _____ Students who have a math and science background as well as skills in information technology will be more marketable.

   B. _____ Most of the 1.6 million high-tech jobs created in the United States in the previous year were filled.

   C. _____ The critical shortage of IT workers is compared to a lack of iron ore in the Industrial Revolution.

   D. _____ U.S. students would achieve more if teachers had higher expectations for them.

   E. _____ The United States needs stepped-up training programs in information technology.

   F. _____ Kindergarten is too early to launch technology training.

3. Do you think the United States will continue to lose ground to other countries in the creation of IT jobs? Why or why not? What changes need to be made in the education system in order to improve training in math and science? Is there a panacea for this educational problem?

INFOTRAC® Research Activity
COLLEGE EDITION
The Online Library

A great deal of research has been done on the influence of birth order on people's behavior. Find articles about the subject by typing in "birth order and personality" and "sibling rivalry and behavior" in the InfoTrac College Edition online library. Read several articles on the subject. What are some characteristics of oldest, middle, and youngest children? Who are some famous people who belong to each group? Does the behavior of these people validate the theory that birth order influences personality? Do you think sibling rivalry between children causes lasting rifts in families, or do the rifts diminish after childhood? **Write a journal entry or composition** explaining your opinion of the importance of birth order. Give examples from the readings as well as from your own family or observation of other families.

UNIT 2

INFLUENCES ON OUR LIVES: NATURE VERSUS NURTURE

Who Lives Longer?

Prereading Preparation

1. In groups of three or four, speculate on how long the average person lives. Discuss factors that affect a person's longevity, both positively and negatively. For example, diet is a factor. What you eat may positively or negatively affect your longevity. Use the chart below to help you organize your ideas.

FACTORS	Positive	Negative
diet		

2. After you have organized the factors, prepare a brief (two or three minute) report that one of you will present to the class.

3. After all the groups in the class have presented their views, work in your group again. Review your chart; make any revisions you want, and then report your group's factors to the class.

4. Read the title of this article. Who do you think the article will say lives longer?

Who Lives Longer?

by Patricia Skalka
McCall's

1   How to live longer is a topic that has fascinated mankind for centuries. Today, scientists are beginning to separate the facts from the fallacies surrounding the aging process. Why is it that some people reach a ripe old age and others do not? Several factors influencing longevity are set at birth, but

5   surprisingly, many others are elements that can be changed. Here is what you should know.

Some researchers divide the elements determining who will live longer into two categories: fixed factors and changeable factors. Gender, race and heredity are fixed factors—they can't be reversed, although certain long-term social

10 changes can influence them. For example, women live longer than men—at birth, their life expectancy is about seven to eight years more. However, cigarette smoking, drinking and reckless driving could shorten this advantage. There is increasing evidence that length of life is also influenced by a number of elements that are within your ability to control. The most obvious

15 are physical lifestyle factors.

Health Measures

According to a landmark study of nearly 7,000 adults in Alameda County, California, women can add up to seven years to their lives and men 11 to 12 years by following seven simple health practices: (1) Don't smoke. (2) If you drink, do so only moderately. (3) Eat breakfast regularly. (4) Don't eat between meals.

20 (5) Maintain normal weight. (6) Sleep about eight hours a night. (7) Exercise moderately.

Cutting calories may be the single most significant lifestyle change you can make. Experiments have shown that in laboratory animals, a 40 percent calorie reduction leads to a 50 percent extension in longevity. "Eating less has a more

25 profound and diversified effect on the aging process than does any other life-

style change," says Byung P. Yu, Ph.D., professor of physiology at the University of Texas Health Science Center at San Antonio. "It is the only factor we know of in laboratory animals that is an anti-aging factor."

Psychosocial Factors

A long life, however, is not just the result of being good to your body and staving off disease. All the various factors that constitute and influence daily life can be critical too. In searching for the ingredients to a long, healthy existence, scientists are studying links between longevity and the psychological and social aspects of human existence. The following can play significant roles in determining your longevity:

Social Integration

Researchers have found that people who are socially integrated—they are part of a family network, are married, participate in structured group activities—live longer.

Early studies indicated that the more friends and relatives you had, the longer you lived. Newer studies focus on the types of relationships that are most beneficial. "Larger networks don't always seem to be advantageous to women," says epidemiologist Teresa Seeman, Ph.D., associate research scientist at Yale University. "Certain kinds of ties add more demands rather than generate more help."

Autonomy

A feeling of autonomy or control can come from having a say in important decisions (where you live, how you spend your money) or from being surrounded by people who inspire confidence in your ability to master certain tasks (yes, you can quit smoking, you will get well). Studies show these feelings bring a sense of well-being and satisfaction with life. "Autonomy is a key factor in successful aging," says Toni Antonucci, associate research scientist at the Institute for Social Research at the University of Michigan.

Stress and Job Satisfaction

Researchers disagree on how these factors affect longevity. There isn't enough data available to support a link between stress and longevity, says Edward L. Schneider, M.D., dean of the Andrus Gerontology Center at the University of Southern California. Animal research, however, provides exciting insights. In studies with laboratory rats, certain types of stress damage the immune system and destroy brain cells, especially those involved in memory.

Other kinds of stress enhance immune function by 20 to 30 percent, supporting a theory first advanced by Hans Selye, M.D., Ph.D., a pioneer in stress research. He proposed that an exciting, active and meaningful life contributes to good health.

The relationship between job satisfaction and longevity also remains in question. According to some researchers, a satisfying job adds years to a man's life, while volunteer work increases a woman's longevity. These findings may change as more women participate in the workforce. One study found that clerical workers suffered twice as many heart attacks as homemakers. Factors associated with the coronary problems were suppressed hostility, having a nonsupportive boss, and decreased job mobility.

Environment

Where you live can make a difference in how long you live. A study by the California Department of Health Services in Berkeley found a 40 percent higher mortality rate among people living in a poverty area compared to those in a nonpoverty area. "The difference was not due to age, sex, health care or life-style," says George A. Kaplan, Ph.D., chief of the department's Human Population Laboratory. The resulting hypothesis: A locale can have environmental characteristics, such as polluted air or water, or socioeconomic characteristics, such as a high crime rate and level of stress, that make it unhealthy.

Socioeconomic Status

People with higher incomes, more education and high-status occupations tend to live longer. Researchers used to think this was due to better living and job conditions, nutrition and access to health care, but these theories have not held up. Nevertheless, the differences can be dramatic. Among women 65 to 74 years old, those with less than an eighth-grade education are much more likely to die than are women who have completed at least one year of college.

What Can You Do

The message from the experts is clear. There are many ways to add years to your life. Instituting sound health practices and expanding your circle of acquaintances and activities will have a beneficial effect. The good news about aging, observes Erdman B. Palmore of the Center for the Study of Aging and Human Development at Duke Medical Center in North Carolina, is many of the factors related to longevity are also related to life satisfaction.

Read the passage again. As you read, underline what you think are the most important ideas in the reading. Then, in one or two sentences, write the main idea of the reading. *Use your own words.*

Main Idea

_____

_____

_____

Details

Complete the chart below to organize the information in the article. Refer back to the information you underlined in the passage as a guide. When you have finished, write a brief summary of the reading. *Use your own words.*

WHO LIVES LONGER?

_____	Changeable Factors	
	_____	_____
A. gender	1.	1.
B.	2.	2.
C.	3.	3.
	4.	4.
	5.	5.
	6.	
	7.	
What you can do: A. B.		

Summary

_____

_____

_____

_____

Statement Evaluation

Read the following statements. Then scan the article again quickly to find out if each sentence is **True (T), False (F),** or **Not Mentioned (NM)** in the article.

1. _____ There is nothing you can do to increase longevity.

2. _____ Laboratory rats that exercised lived longer than those that did not exercise.

3. _____ Eating less may help you live longer.

4. _____ There may be a connection between longevity and psychological factors.

5. _____ Women who work outside the home have more heart attacks than working men do.

6. _____ People who live in poverty areas live longer than people who live in nonpoverty areas.

7. _____ People with higher socioeconomic status tend to live longer than those with lower socioeconomic status.

Reading Analysis

Read each question carefully. Either circle the letter or number of the correct answer or write your answer in the space provided.

1. a. Read lines 1–3. Which word means the opposite of **fact**?

    _____

    b. How do you know?

    _____

2. Read lines 3–4. People who **"reach a ripe old age"** are people who
    a. die young
    b. are women
    c. live a long time

3. Read lines 8–10. **Fixed factors** are those that
    a. we can change
    b. we are born with
    c. can be reversed

4. In lines 9, 10, and 35, what follows the dashes (—)?
    a. Explanations
    b. Causes
    c. New ideas

5. Read lines 8–12. What are examples of **certain long-term social changes**?

    _____

6. Read lines 18–19. **"If you drink, do so only moderately."** What does this sentence about alcohol mean?
    a. Do not drink.
    b. Drink as much as you want.
    c. Only drink a little.

7. Read lines 33–34. What does **the following** refer to?

   _____

8. Read lines 44–47. **Having a say** means
   a. having an opinion
   b. having a choice
   c. speaking loudly

9. Read line 51. What do **these factors** refer to?

   _____

10. Read lines 64–67. **Coronary problems** are
    a. hostility
    b. dissatisfaction with your job
    c. heart attacks

11. Read lines 73–75. What is a **hypothesis**?
    a. A theory
    b. A fact
    c. A law

D. DICTIONARY SKILLS

Read the entry for each word, and consider the context of the sentence from the passage. Write the number of the definition that is appropriate for the context on the line next to the word. Be prepared to explain your choice.

1. The study of nearly 7,000 adults in California was a **landmark** in the field of health. According to the study, women can add up to seven years to their lives and men 11 to 12 years by following seven simple health practices.

   landmark: _____

   > **land·mark** \-ˌmärk\ *n* (bef. 12c) **1 :** an object (as a stone or tree) that marks the boundary of land **2 a :** a conspicuous object on land that marks a locality **b :** an anatomical structure used as a point of orientation in locating other structures **3 :** an event or development that marks a turning point or a stage **4 :** a structure (as a building) of unusual historical and usu. aesthetic interest; *esp* : one that is officially designated and set aside for preservation

2. Eating less has a more **profound** effect on the aging process than does any other lifestyle change. It is the only factor we know of in laboratory animals that is an anti-aging factor.

   profound: _____

   > **pro·found** \prə'faůnd, prō-\ *adj* [ME, fr. MF *profond* deep, fr. L *profundus,* fr. *pro-* before + *fundus* bottom — more at PRO-, BOTTOM] (14c) **1 a :** having intellectual depth and insight **b :** difficult to fathom or understand **2 a :** extending far below the suface **b :** coming from, reaching to, or situated at a depth : DEEP-SEATED ⟨a ~ sigh⟩ **3 a :** characterized by intensity of feeling or quality **b :** all encompassing : COMPLETE ⟨~ sleep⟩ — **pro·found·ly** \-'faůn(d)-lē\ *adv* — **pro·found·ness** \-'faůn(d),-nəs \ *n*

\ə\abut \ə\ kitten, \ər\ further \a\ ash \ā\ ace \ä\ mop, mar \aů \ out \ch\ chin \e\ bet \ē\ easy \g\go \i\ hit \ī\ ice \j\job \ŋ\sing \ō\ go \o\ law \oi\ boy \th\ thin \th\ the \ü\ loot \ů\ foot \y\ yet \zh\ vision \ȧ, k, ⁿ, œ, œ̄, ɶ, ɶ̄, ʸ\ *See Website below for* Pronunciation Guide.

By permission. From *Merriam-Webster's Online Dictionary* ©2002 by Merriam-Webster, Incorporated (www.Merriam-Webster.com).

3. A feeling of autonomy or control can come from having a **say** in important decisions (where you live, how you spend your money).

say: _____

> **say** *n, pl* **says** \'sāz. *Southern also* 'sez\
> (1571) **1** *archaic* : something that is said :
> STATEMENT **2 :** an expression of opinion
> ⟨had my ~⟩ **3 :** a right or power to influence
> action or decision; *esp* : the authority to
> make final decisions

4. Instituting **sound** health practices and expanding your circle of acquaintances and activities will have a beneficial effect.

sound: _____

> **sound** \'saund\ *adj* [ME, fr. OE *gesund;* akin
> to OHG *gisunt* healthy] (13c)
> **1 a :** free from injury or disease : exhibiting
> normal health **b :** free from flaw, defect, or
> decay ⟨~ timber⟩ **2 :** SOLID, FIRM; *also* :
> STABLE **3 a :** free from error, fallacy,
> or misapprehension ⟨~ reasoning⟩
> **b :** exhibiting or based on thorough
> knowledge and experience ⟨~ scholarship⟩
> **c :** legally valid ⟨a ~ title⟩ **d :** logically
> valid and having true premises **e :** agreeing
> with accepted views : ORTHODOX
> **4 a :** THOROUGH **b :** deep and undisturbed
> ⟨a ~ sleep⟩ **c :** HARD, SEVERE ⟨a ~ whipping⟩
> **5 :** showing good judgment or sense *syn* see
> HEALTHY, VALID— **sound·ly** \'saun(d)-lē\ *adv*
> — **sound·ness** \'saun(d)-nəs\ *n*

E. Critical Thinking Strategies

Read each question carefully. Write your response in the space provided. Remember that there is no one correct answer. Your response depends on what **you** think.

1. What tone does the author set at the end of the article? Is she upbeat, pessimistic, matter-of-fact, etc.?

   _____

   _____

2. Does the author of "Who Lives Longer?" believe that increasing life expectancy is a desirable goal? Explain your answer.

   _____

   _____

3. Why does eating have such a dramatic positive effect on longevity?

   _____

   _____

4. Why do you think volunteer work increases a woman's longevity?

   _____

   _____

5. How are clerical workers and homemakers similar? Why do you think clerical workers suffer twice as many heart attacks as homemakers?

   _____

   _____

Another Perspective

More Senior Citizens, Fewer Kids

by Jessie Cheng
Free China Review

1   "Thirty years from now, it will be rare to see children walking along the streets of Taiwan," says Chen Kuanjeng, a research fellow in the Institute of Sociology at Academia Sinica. "Instead, the streets will be full of elderly people." Chen's prediction may sound a bit drastic, but he voices a growing concern

5   among sociologists over the dramatic shift under way in Taiwan society toward a graying population. As in many developed countries, island families are having fewer children, while at the same time the average life span is increasing to create a larger and larger pool of senior citizens.

Between 1953 and 1993, the annual birthrate declined from about forty-five

10   births per thousand persons to less than sixteen. During the same period, the average number of children per Taiwan couple declined by more than two-thirds, from 7 to 1.7. The current average is below that of the United States (2 children per couple), mainland China (1.9), and Britain or France (both 1.8). The Taiwan

figure also means that since 1984 the birthrate has dropped below the "replacement level." Sociologists predict that within forty years, the total population will be declining.

Another trend is also changing the face of Taiwan's population: the average life span is steadily rising, leading to a growing proportion of elderly people. In 1951, local men lived an average of 53 years, and women lived 56 years. Today, men average 72 years and women 77. Because the trend toward fewer children and more senior citizens is expected to continue, sociologists predict that the elderly proportion of the population will increase steadily. While persons aged over 65 made up just over 7 percent of the population in 1994, they are expected to account for 22 percent by the year 2036—a figure that could mean more than five million senior citizens.

The result is an overall "graying" of society and a new set of social welfare needs that must be met—nursing homes rather than nursery schools, day care programs for the elderly rather than for preschoolers. Social scientists predict these demands will be hard to fulfill. "In the future, there won't be enough young people to support the older people," says Chen. Sociologists are particularly concerned that expanding health care costs for senior citizens will mean a large financial burden for taxpayers. Another concern is that a dwindling population of working-age adults will slow economic growth.

Patterns in Taiwan's population growth looked far different just a generation ago. During the 1950s, the island's population zoomed from 7.6 million to a 1960 figure of 10.8 million. The centuries-old belief that more children bring luck to a family was strong among local residents.

But as the decade came to a close, the rapid population increase began to alarm sociologists. Opposition notwithstanding, the government launched a pre-pregnancy health campaign in 1959 which included teaching birth control methods through public hospitals and health stations (community out-patient clinics). Still, Taiwan's population grew from 14.7 million to 17.8 million during the 1970s, and social scientists continued to urge further population control measures.

The 1980s marked a turning point in population control. In addition to official family planning campaigns, a number of social factors have led to the declining birthrate. For example, couples are marrying later, and a growing number of young people are opting to stay single.

But sociologists worry that population control measures have gone too far. The government is now reversing its official stance on family planning. "While in past decades we controlled the population, over the next few years we will promote a reasonable growth rate," says Chien Tai-lang, director of the Department of Population, Ministry of the Interior.

1. Which two important population factors in Taiwan does this article discuss?

   _____

   _____

2. How are these factors expected to affect Taiwan in the future?

   _____

   _____

3. What potential problems might this population shift create?

   _____

   _____

   _____

4. Why is the birthrate declining?

   _____

   _____

   _____

Follow-up Activities

1. Refer to the **Self-Evaluation of Reading Strategies** on page 137. Think about the strategies you used to help yourself understand "Who Lives Longer?" Check off the strategies you used. Think about the strategies you didn't use, and try to apply them to help yourself understand the readings that follow.

2. Look at the following chart carefully; then answer the related questions.

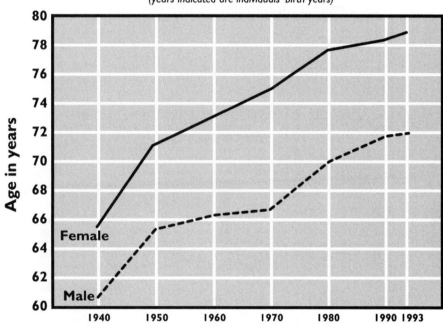

Life Expectancy in the United States
(years indicated are individuals' birth years)

a. What does this chart illustrate?

    _____

b. 1. About how long can a female born in 1970 expect to live?

        _____

    2. About how long can a male born in 1970 expect to live?

        _____

c. 1. In what decade did life expectancy for males make the greatest gain? How many years did males gain?

        _____

2. In what decade did life expectancy for females make the greatest gain? How many years did females gain?

_____

3. In general terms, speculate on what could account for this great increase in life expectancy for *both* sexes in this particular decade.

_____

_____

_____

d. 1. Between 1940 and 1993, what was the overall gain in life expectancy for males?

_____

2. Between 1940 and 1993, what was the overall gain in life expectancy for females?

_____

3. Look at the following chart carefully; then answer the related questions.

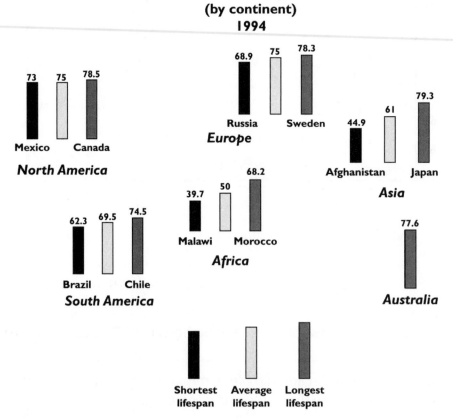

World Lifespan Highs and Lows
(by continent)
1994

a. What does this chart illustrate?

_____

_____

b. What are some factors that might account for such a worldwide range in life expectancy, e.g., from 39.7 in Malawi or 44.9 in Afghanistan to 79.3 in Japan or 78.3 in Sweden?

_____

_____

4. Work with a partner. Plan a healthy diet for yourselves. Compare your diet with your classmates' diets. As a class, decide which diet is the healthiest.

5. Work with a partner to design a survey to try to predict life expectancy, using the factors that have a positive or negative effect. Include questions about personal behavior (for example, "Do you smoke?"). Ask your classmates and/or other interviewees to respond to your survey. Afterwards you will try to predict how long these people will live. Also, for each person, suggest two changes you believe would result in greater longevity for that person.

H. Topics for Discussion AND Writing

1. What are some of the consequences of an aging population? In other words, what factors must be taken into consideration as the elderly begin to make up a larger segment of a country's population than ever before? What needs will have to be met?

2. In your group, discuss the factors that might shorten a person's life expectancy.

3. Work with two or three other students. In your group, make a list of the steps you can take to increase your life expectancy.

4. Refer to the "World Lifespan Highs and Lows" chart on page 92. Choose a country from the chart. Write a composition about the life expectancy in this country. Include what you think may be reasons for this country's high or low life expectancy.

5. **Write in your journal.** How long would you like to live? Explain your reasons.

I. Cloze Quiz

Chapter 4: Who Lives Longer?

Read the passage below. Fill in the blanks with one word from the list.
Use each word only once.

ability	evidence	heredity	longevity	ripe
birth	expectancy	influence	maintain	separate
changeable	fallacies	landmark	moderately	shorten
elements	health	longer	reversed	years

How to live _____ is a topic that has fascinated mankind for
(1)
centuries. Today, scientists are beginning to _____ the facts
(2)
from the _____ surrounding the aging process. Why is it that
(3)
some people reach a _____ old age and others do not? Several
(4)
factors influencing _____ are set at _____, but
(5)   (6)
surprisingly, many others are elements that can be changed. Here is what
you should know.

Some researchers divide the _____ determining who will
(7)
live longer into two categories: fixed factors and _____ factors.
(8)
Gender, race and _____ are fixed factors—they can't be
(9)
_____, although certain long-term social changes can
(10)
_____ them. For example, women live longer than men—at
(11)
birth, their life _____ is about seven to eight years more.
(12)
However, cigarette smoking, drinking and reckless driving could
_____ this advantage.
(13)

There is increasing _____ that length of life is also
                              (14)
influenced by a number of elements that are within your _____
                                                                    (15)
to control. The most obvious are physical lifestyle factors.

Health Measures

According to a _____ study of nearly 7,000 adults in
                        (16)
Alameda County, California, women can add up to seven _____
                                                                   (17)
to their lives and men 11 to 12 years by following seven simple

_____ practices: Don't smoke. If you drink, do so only
        (18)
_____. Eat breakfast regularly. Don't eat between meals.
        (19)
_____ normal weight. Sleep about eight hours a night. Exercise
        (20)
moderately.

5

The Mindset of Health

Prereading Preparation

1. In a small group, look at the photographs of the doctors with their patients, on this page and on page 104. Consider each doctor's demeanor, or behavior, with his patient, and each patient's apparent attitude. What differences do you perceive? How do you think these differences affect the doctor/patient relationship in each case? What do you think about the attitude of each patient towards his treatment?

2. What factors influence good health or bad health? In your group, make a list of factors. When you are finished, compare your list with your classmates' lists. What can you add to your list?

Factors Contributing to Good Health	Factors Contributing to Bad Health

3. A **mindset** is an emotional attitude that influences how a person responds to a situation. What do you think **the mindset of health** means? How might it affect our health?

4. Imagine that you are not feeling well, so you visit your doctor. In your group, describe your office visit in terms of your conversation with your doctor. For example, do you go alone or with someone else? Do you ask the doctor questions if you don't understand? Do you ask about alternative treatments to the one the doctor prescribes? When each of you has described your hypothetical doctor's visit, decide whether your attitude towards your doctor resembles the one you described for the patient on page 97, on page 104, or someone different. When you have finished, decide as a group on the most effective way to talk with your doctor. Discuss your decision with the class. What did you all agree on?

5. Read the title of this passage. What do you think this article will be about?

The Mindset of Health

by Ellen J. Langer
Mindfulness

Consider this scenario: During a routine physical, your doctor notices a small lump and orders a biopsy as a cancer-screening measure. Your immediate reaction is fear, probably intense fear. Yet in some cases, a tiny lump or mole requires only a tiny incision, comparable to removing a large splinter. Fear in such a situation is based not on the procedure but on your interpretation of what the doctor is doing. You're not thinking about splinters or minor cuts; you're thinking biopsy, cancer, death.

From earliest childhood we learn to see mind and body as separate—and to regard the body as without question the more essential of the two. And later, we take our physical problems to one sort of doctor, our mental problems to another. But the mind/body split is not only one of our strongest beliefs, it is a dangerous and premature psychological commitment.

When we think of various influences on our health, we tend to think of many of them as coming from the outside environment. But each outside influence is mediated by context. Our perceptions and interpretations influence the ways in which our bodies respond to information in the world. If we automatically—"mindlessly"—accept preconceived notions of the context of a particular situation, we can jeopardize the body's ability to handle that situation. Sometimes, for the sake of our health, we need to place our perceptions intentionally, that is, mindfully in a different context.

Context can be so powerful that it influences our basic needs. In an experiment on hunger, subjects who chose to fast for a prolonged time for personal reasons tended to be less hungry than those who fasted for external reasons—for money, for example. Freely choosing to perform a task means that one has adopted a certain attitude toward it. In this experiment, those who had made a personal psychological commitment not only were less hungry, but they also showed a smaller increase in free fatty acid levels, a physiological indicator of hunger. The obvious conclusion: State of mind shapes state of body.

A wide body of recent research has been devoted to investigating the influence of attitudes on the immune system, which is thought to be the intermediary between psychological states and physical illness. The emotional context, our interpretation of the events around us, could thus be the first link in a chain leading to serious illness. And since context is something we can control, the clarification of these links between psychology and illness is good news. Diseases that were once thought to be purely physiological and probably incurable may be more amenable to personal control than we once believed.

Even when a disease may appear to progress inexorably, our reactions to it can be mindful or mindless and thus influence its effects. A very common mindset, as mentioned before, is the conviction that cancer means death. Even if a tumor has not yet had any effect on any body function, or how you feel physically, rarely will you think of yourself as healthy after having a malignancy diagnosed. At the same time, there are almost certainly people walking around with undiagnosed cancer who consider themselves healthy, and may remain so. Yet many doctors have noticed that, following a diagnosis of cancer, some patients seem to go into a decline that has little to do with the actual course of the disease. But they needn't. By reinterpreting the context, they might avoid the unnecessary failure attributable to fear alone.

In recent years there has been much new research that now supports the value of a mindful approach in handling a variety of health situations such as pain. Patients have been successfully taught to tolerate rather severe pain by seeing how pain varies depending on context (thinking of bruises incurred during a football game that are easily tolerated, versus the attention we require to nurse a mere paper cut).

This mindful exercise helped the patients get by with fewer pain relievers and sedatives and to leave the hospital earlier than a comparison group of patients. And the results seem to indicate more than a simple, temporary distraction of the mind, because once the stimulus—the source of pain—has been reinterpreted so that the person has a choice of context, one painful, one not, the mind is unlikely to return to the original interpretation. It has, in effect, changed contexts.

We all know people who have quit smoking "cold turkey." Do they succeed because their commitment to stop put withdrawal symptoms into a new context? Jonathan Margolis, a graduate student at Harvard, and I explored this question in two stages. First we tried to find out if smokers in a nonsmoking context experienced strong cravings for cigarettes. We questioned smokers in three situations that prohibited smoking: in a movie theater, at work, and on a religious holiday. The results in each setting were very similar. People did not suffer withdrawal symptoms when they were in any of the nonsmoking contexts. But when they returned to a context where smoking was allowed—a smoke break at work, for instance—their cravings resurfaced.

All of these people escaped the urge to smoke in a mindless manner. Could they have achieved the same thing deliberately? Can people control the experience of temptation?

People who want to stop smoking usually remind themselves of the health risks, the bad smell, the cost, others' reactions to their smoking—the drawbacks of smoking. But these effects are not the reasons they smoke, so trying to quit for those reasons alone often leads to failure. The problem is that all of the positive aspects of smoking are still there and still have strong appeal—the relaxation, the concentration, the taste, the sociable quality of smoking.

A more mindful approach would be to look carefully at these pleasures and find other, less harmful ways of obtaining them. If the needs served by an addiction or habit can be satisfied in different ways, it would be easier to shake. The deliberate nature of mindfulness is what makes its potential so enormous.

Whenever we try to heal ourselves and do not abdicate this responsibility completely to doctors, each step is mindful. We welcome new information, whether from our bodies or from books. We look at our illness from more than the single perspective of medicine. We work on changing contexts, whether it is a stressful workplace or a depressing view of the hospital. And finally, when we attempt to stay healthy rather than to be made well, we become involved in the process rather than the outcome.

There are two ways in which we have learned to influence our health: exchanging unhealthy mindsets for healthy ones and increasing a generally mindful state. The latter method is more lasting and results in more personal control. Understanding the importance of abandoning the mind/body dualism that has shaped both our thinking and the practice of medicine for so long can make a profound difference in both what we do and how we feel.

Consider how you learned to ride a bike. Someone older held on to the seat as you pedaled to keep you from falling until you found your balance. Then, without your knowledge, that strong hand let go and you were riding on your own. You controlled the bicycle without even knowing you had learned how.

The same is true for all of us most of our lives. We control our health, and the course of disease, without really knowing that we do. But just as on the bike, at some point we all discover that we are in control. Now may be the time for many of us to learn how to recognize and use the control we possess over illness through mindfulness.

Read the passage again. As you read, underline what you think are the most important ideas in the reading. Then, in one or two sentences, write the main idea of the reading. *Use your own words.*

Main Idea

_____

_____

_____

Details

Use the flowchart on the next page to organize the information in the article. Refer back to the information you underlined in the passage as a guide. When you have finished, write a brief summary of the reading. *Use your own words.*

THE MINDSET OF HEALTH

The Significance of Mindful Attitudes

```
┌──────────────────────────────────┐
│            Context               │
│                                  │
│                                  │
└──────────────────────────────────┘
              ↓
┌──────────────────────────────────┐
│          State of Mind           │
│                                  │
│                                  │
└──────────────────────────────────┘
```

The Significance of Mindless Attitudes

```
┌──────────────────────────────────┐
│            Context               │
│                                  │
│                                  │
└──────────────────────────────────┘
              ↓
┌──────────────────────────────────┐
│          State of Mind           │
│                                  │
│                                  │
└──────────────────────────────────┘
```

```
┌────────────────────────────────────────────────────────┐
│ The importance of context and mindfulness in handling illness │
│ 1.                                                       │
│                                                          │
│ 2.                                                       │
│                                                          │
│ 3.                                                       │
│                                                          │
│         a.                                               │
│                                                          │
│         b.                                               │
└────────────────────────────────────────────────────────┘
                           ↓
┌────────────────────────────────────────────────────────┐
│      Research supporting the effects of mindfulness      │
│ 1.                                                       │
│                                                          │
│ 2.                                                       │
└────────────────────────────────────────────────────────┘
                           ↓
┌────────────────────────────────────────────────────────┐
│      How to take a more mindful approach to illness      │
│ 1.                                                       │
│ 2.                                                       │
│ 3.                                                       │
│ 4.                                                       │
└────────────────────────────────────────────────────────┘
                           ↓
┌────────────────────────────────────────────────────────┐
│          How to positively influence our health         │
│ 1.                                                       │
│ 2.                                                       │
│                                                          │
│                                                          │
└────────────────────────────────────────────────────────┘
```

Summary

_____

_____

_____

_____

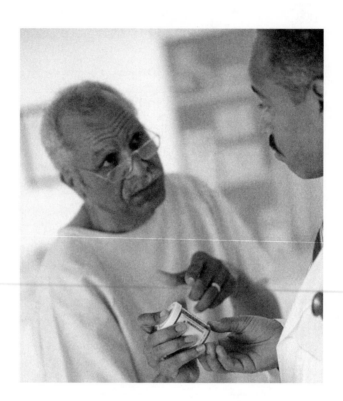

B. Statement Evaluation

Read the following statements. Then scan the article again quickly to find out if each sentence is **True (T), False (F),** or an **Inference (I).**

1. _____ The people who chose to fast for money were hungrier than those who chose to fast for personal reasons.

2. _____ Researchers have found a clear connection between attitude and illness.

3. _____ New research indicates that a mindful approach may help people handle pain.

4. _____ When smokers were in nonsmoking contexts, they had the urge to smoke.

5. _____ Our mindset influences our health.

6. _____ The way you think sends messages that influence how your body responds.

7. _____ People who quit smoking did not have cigarette cravings in nonsmoking contexts because of their mindset.

Read each question carefully. Either circle the letter or number of the correct answer or write your answer in the space provided.

1. Read lines 16–19.
   a. What word is a synonym of **automatically**?

   _____

   b. These two words mean
      1. carelessly
      2. purposely
      3. without thinking

2. Read lines 19–20.
   a. What word is a synonym of **intentionally**?

   _____

   b. These two synonyms mean
      1. carelessly
      2. purposely
      3. without thinking
   c. What follows **that is** in this sentence?
      1. An explanation of the previous idea
      2. A contrasting idea
      3. A new idea

3. Read lines 21–28.
   a. What does **to fast** mean?
      1. To not eat
      2. To eat
      3. To go quickly
   b. Read "**In an experiment on hunger . . . for example.**" In this sentence, what is **money** an example of?

   _____

c. In this experiment, how did researchers know which subjects were less hungry?

_____

4. Read lines 50–53. What does **versus** mean?
    a. In addition to
    b. In contrast with
    c. The same as

5. Read lines 56–59.
    a. What is the **stimulus**?

    _____

    b. How do you know?

    _____

6. Read lines 65–67. What follows the colon (:)?
    a. Examples
    b. Opinions
    c. Places

7. Read lines 74–79.

    a. What are the **drawbacks of smoking**?

    _____

    b. What are the **positive aspects of smoking**?

    _____

    c. What is a **drawback**?
        1. An expense
        2. A risk
        3. A disadvantage

8. Read lines 91–94. The **latter method** refers to
    a. exchanging unhealthy mindsets for healthy ones
    b. increasing a generally mindful state

D. DICTIONARY SKILLS

Read the entry for each word, and consider the context of the sentence from the passage. Write the number of the definition that is appropriate for the context on the line next to the word. Be prepared to explain your choice.

1. A large **body** of recent research has been devoted to investigating attitude and the immune system.

    body: _____

    > **body** \'bä-dē\ *n, pl* **bod·ies** [ME, fr. OE *bodig;* akin to OHG *boteh* corpse] (bef. 12c)
    > **1 a :** the main part of a plant or animal body esp. as distinguished from limbs and head : TRUNK **b :** the main, central, or principal part: as (1) : the nave of a church (2) : the bed or box of a vehicle on or in which the load is placed (3) : the enclosed or partly enclosed part of an automobile **2 a :** the organized physical substance of an animal or plant either living or dead: as (1) : the material part or nature of a human being (2) : the dead organism : CORPSE **b :** a human being : PERSON **3 a :** a mass of matter distinct from other masses ⟨a ~ of water⟩ ⟨a celestial ~⟩ **b :** something that embodies or gives concrete reality to a thing; *also* : a sensible object in physical space **c :** AGGREGATE, QUANTITY ⟨a ~ of evidence⟩ **4 a :** the part of a garment covering the body or trunk **b :** the main part of a literary or journalistic work : TEXT 2b **c :** the sound box or pipe of a musical instrument **5 :** a group of persons or things: as **a :** a fighting unit : FORCE **b :** a group of individuals organized for some purpose ⟨a legislative ~⟩ **6 a :** fullness and richness of flavor (as of wine) **b :** VISCOSITY, CONSISTENCY — used esp. of oils and grease **c :** compactness or firmness of texture **d :** fullness or resonance of a musical tone

2. In an experiment on hunger, subjects who chose to fast for a prolonged time for personal reasons tended to be less hungry than those who fasted for external reasons—for money, for example. Freely choosing to perform a task means that one has adopted a certain attitude toward it. In this experiment, those who had made a personal psychological **commitment** were less hungry than the others.

    commitment: _____

    > **com·mit·ment** \kə-'mitmənt\ *n* (1621)
    > **1 a :** an act of committing to a charge or trust: as (1) : a consignment to a penal or mental institution (2) : an act of referring a matter to a legislative committee **b :** MITTIMUS **2 a :** an agreement or pledge to do something in the future; *esp* : an engagement to assume a financial obligation at a future date **b :** something pledged **c :** the state or an instance of being obligated or emotionally impelled ⟨a ~ to a cause⟩

\ə\abut \ᵊ\ kitten, \ər\ further \a\ ash \ā\ ace \ä\ mop, mar \aú\ out \ch\ chin \e\ bet \ē\ easy \g\go \i\ hit \ī\ ice \j\job \ŋ\sing \ō\ go \ò\ law \òi\ boy \th\ thin \th\ the \ü\ loot \ú\ foot \y\ yet \zh\ vision \á, k, ⁿ, œ, œ̄, ᵫ, ᵫ̄, ʸ\ *See Website below for* Pronunciation Guide.

By permission. From *Merriam-Webster's Online Dictionary* ©2002 by Merriam-Webster, Incorporated (www.Merriam-Webster.com).

3. We control our health, and the **course** of illness, without really knowing that we do. In fact, many doctors have noticed that, following a diagnosis of cancer, some patients seem to go into a decline that has little to do with the actual **course** of the disease.

course: _____

> **course** \'kōrs, 'kȯrs\ *n* [ME, fr. OF, fr. L *cursus*, fr. *currere* to run — more at CAR] (14c) **1 :** the act or action of moving in a path from point to point **2 :** the path over which something moves or extends: as **a :** RACECOURSE **b** (1) : the direction of travel of a vehicle (as a ship or airplane) usu. measured as a clockwise angle from north; *also :* the projected path of travel (2) : a point of the compass **c :** WATERCOURSE **d :** GOLF COURSE **3 a :** accustomed procedure or normal action ⟨the law taking its ~⟩ **b :** a chosen manner of conducting oneself : way of acting ⟨our wisest ~ is to retreat⟩ **c** (1) : progression through a development or period or a series of acts or events (2) : LIFE HISTORY, CAREER **4 :** an ordered process or succession: as **a :** a number of lectures or other matter dealing with a subject; *also :* a series of such courses constituting a curriculum ⟨a premed ~⟩ **b :** a series of doses or medications administered over a designated period **5 a :** a part of a meal served at one time **b :** LAYER; *esp :* a continuous level range of brick or masonry throughout a wall **c :** the lowest sail on a square-rigged mast — **in due course :** after a normal passage of time : in the expected or allotted time — **of course 1 :** following the ordinary way or procedure **2 :** as might be expected

4. Our perceptions influence how our bodies respond to information in the world. If we automatically—"mindlessly"—accept preconceived **notions** of the context of a particular situation, we can jeopardize the body's ability to handle that situation.

notion:

_____

> **no·tion** \'nō-'shən\ *n* [L *notion-, notio,* fr. *noscere*] (1537) **1 a** (1) : an individual's conception or impression of something known, experienced, or imagined (2) : an inclusive general concept (3) : a theory or belief held by a person or group **b :** a personal inclination : WHIM **2** *obs :* MIND, INTELLECT **3** *pl :* small useful items : SUNDRIES *syn* see IDEA

E. Critical Thinking

Read each question carefully. Write your response in the space provided. Remember that there is no one correct answer. Your response depends on what **you** think.

1. Read this sentence: "The emotional context, our interpretation of the events around us, could thus be the first link in a chain leading to serious illness." The author is comparing links in a chain in order to describe the chain of events from our emotional context to a serious illness. What do you think this chain of events is? How can this chain of events be broken at any given step on the way to serious illness?

    _____

    _____

    _____

    _____

2. Read this sentence: "Diseases that were once thought to be purely physiological and probably incurable may be more amenable to personal control than we once believed." What kind of effect might personal control have on these diseases? What diseases do you think we might be able to control in this way?

    _____

    _____

    _____

    _____

3. Read the paragraph regarding teaching patients to deal with pain. The author states that these patients were able to "get by with fewer pain relievers and sedatives and to leave the hospital earlier than a comparison group of patients." Who was the other, comparison, group of patients? Why were two groups of patients used in this research? Is this a valid method of research? Why or why not?

    _____

    _____

    _____

    _____

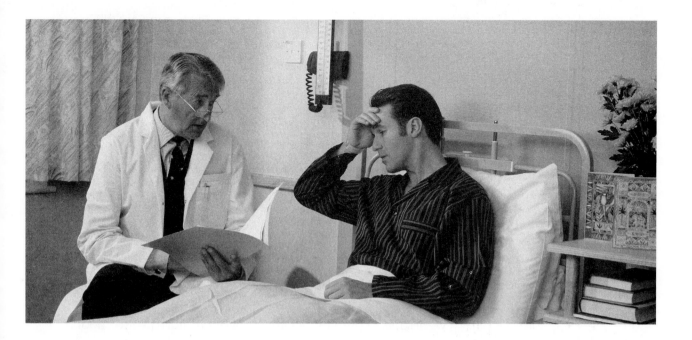

Another Perspective

How to Behave in a Hospital

by Gloria Emerson
American Health

1   Appear to be submissive, humble, grateful and undemanding. Show unbridled pleasure if a doctor comes into your room, even if the visit is brief and useless. Be courteous to all nurses and others on the staff. Give thanks often. Do not challenge anyone with authority unless you are famous, very rich, a
5   member of at least a minor royal family or related to a head of state.

Stay alert. For example, when medicine is handed out, the names of patients are usually written on the bottoms of the paper cups holding the pills. If your name is Walters, do not accept medicine designated for Alvarez. Tactfully point out the mistake, pretending that your eyesight is poor and you
10   may be muddled.

These are a few strategies—offered after 12 days in a hospital in Princeton, N.J., and another 12 days in a huge teaching hospital in New York City—for dealing with today's American medical establishment.

What patients want is to be treated with respect and consideration, which
15   in my experience too few hospitals and doctors bestow. In his book *A Whole New Life*, novelist Reynolds Price recalls that his doctors chose a crowded hallway as

the place to tell him he might have a tumor on his spinal cord. It did not occur to the two physicians that a "hallway mob scene" was not the most appropriate venue for that particular piece of news. Price writes of the "well-known but endlessly deplorable and faceless—near criminal—nature of so much current medicine."

In the operating room of the Princeton hospital where my profoundly fractured hip is to be repaired, I listen to the anesthesiologist chattering to a colleague about the pastrami sandwiches served by a local delicatessen. A few days later, the same anesthesiologist telephones to say that he has seen, in a bookstore, one of the books I have written and wants to know how I feel. I thank him. But he has not fooled me; I know that he mistakenly thinks I'm an important person and wishes only to ingratiate himself.

My surgeon, who is in his mid 30s, looks tired: He has been overwhelmed with patients who have fallen on the treacherous winter ice, his beeper is going off every 15 minutes. He is a witty man, but sometimes his wit is unwelcome.

"Blue Cross[1] wants me to put you out in the snow tomorrow afternoon," he tells me after I have been in the hospital for more than a week. I'm terrified, because I have no idea where to go. I cannot walk, or even lift my leg a few inches. The hospital social worker strikes me as an idiot, but my complaints about her only annoy my surgeon. "I have to work with these people," he tells my friend Dr. Karen Brudney when she mercifully intercedes on my behalf and arranges for me to be transferred to another hospital.

"If you say one negative thing, they get defensive," she tells me later. "They have this kind of institutional loyalty." Brudney told me: "Always bring an advocate—that is, any other person—with you to the hospital, and write everything down, every single question and the answer, the name of every doctor and nurse. When people know you have their names, they behave better."

Since it is not wise to be regarded as a whiner or to be too demanding (the nurses begin to ignore you or take longer in coming to your room) Brudney—my advocate—advises cunning strategies. "You can frame your questions as those of a frightened patient. For example, 'Do you think my foot should really hurt this much?'"

And Brudney adds: "If you, as a patient, suggest that you might like to control even part of the situation or be consulted or informed, then you are considered difficult. They want you to be totally passive. The entire health care system, particularly hospitals and nursing homes, exists for reasons that have nothing to do with taking care of patients. Patients are incidental."

[1]Blue Cross is a major health insurance company.

1. How does Gloria Emerson suggest we behave in a hospital?

   _____

   _____

   _____

2. In a hospital, if someone gives us the wrong medicine, according to Ms. Emerson, how should we react?

   _____

   _____

   _____

3. How do Gloria Emerson and Ellen Langer differ in their ideas about how we should behave in hospitals, or with doctors in general?

   _____

   _____

   _____

G. Follow-up Activities

1. Refer to the **Self-Evaluation of Reading Strategies** on page 137. Think about the strategies you used to help yourself understand "The Mindset of Health." Check off the strategies you used. Think about the strategies you didn't use, and try to apply them to help yourself understand the readings that follow.

2. The tendency in the United States to go to different people for our emotional and physical problems is not universal. Some cultures treat the person holistically. In a small group, compare health care in your country with that in the United States and in the countries of your classmates. How are they similar? How are they different?

3. Work with a partner. One person will act the role of a doctor, and the other person will act the role of a patient. The patient will want to lose weight or stop smoking, or some other reason you choose. Work together to set up a mindful context to help the person achieve this goal. Include specific information about the reason why this person wants to lose weight or stop smoking, as well as which situations the patient should avoid and which situations would be helpful for the patient to be in to help him or her achieve the goal.

4. Work in pairs. Discuss how Gloria Emerson's suggestions for behavior differ from Ellen Langer's. Which approach is mindful? Which approach is mindless? Compare your responses with your classmates'. Do you all have the same responses?

H. *Topics for* Discussion *AND* Writing

1. Researchers are investigating the influence of attitude on the immune system. What effect do you think the mind has on the body? Do you think there is a connection? How are they connected?

2. Gloria Emerson described an atmosphere that is common in many hospitals today. How can we ensure that we are treated well in a hospital and that we get the information about our medication and treatment that we need?

3. **Write in your journal.** Describe a time in your life when you needed medical help. How did you respond emotionally to your illness and to the doctor? Did you have a mindful or a mindless attitude? Do you think you would respond differently now after reading these two articles? Explain your answer.

Cloze Quiz

Chapter 5: The Mindset of Health

Read the passage below. Fill in the blanks with one word from the list.
Use each word only once.

automatically	essential	hungry	link	research
between	experiment	illness	perceptions	separate
body	external	influences	physical	split
control	fast	intentionally	problems	system

From earliest childhood we learn to see mind and body as

_____ and to regard the body as without question the more
(1)

_____ of the two. And later, we take our _____
(2)   (3)

problems to one sort of doctor, our mental _____ to another.
(4)

But the mind/body _____ is not only one of our strongest
(5)

beliefs, it is a dangerous and premature psychological commitment.

When we think of various _____ on our health, we tend to
(6)

think of many of them as coming from the outside environment. But each

outside influence is mediated by context. Our _____ and
(7)

interpretations influence the ways in which our bodies respond to

information in the world. If we _____ —"mindlessly"—accept
(8)

preconceived notions of the context of a particular situation, we can

jeopardize the body's ability to handle that situation. Sometimes, for the sake

of our health, we need to place our perceptions _____, that is,
(9)

mindfully in a different context.

Context can be so powerful that it influences our basic needs. In an

experiment on hunger, subjects who chose to _____ for a
(10)

prolonged time for personal reasons tended to be less hungry than those

who fasted for _____ reasons—for money, for example. Freely
                        (11)

choosing to perform a task means that one has adopted a certain attitude

toward it. In this _____, those who had made a personal
                          (12)

psychological commitment were less _____. The obvious
                                                (13)

conclusion: State of mind shapes state of _____.
                                                      (14)

A wide body of recent _____ has been devoted to
                                (15)

investigating the influence of attitudes on the immune _____,
                                                                    (16)

which is thought to be the intermediary between psychological states and

physical illness. The emotional context, our interpretation of the events

around us, could thus be the first _____ in a chain leading to
                                            (17)

serious _____. And since context is something we can
              (18)

_____, the clarification of these links _____
        (19)   (20)

psychology and illness is good news. Diseases that were once thought to be

purely physiological and probably incurable may be more amenable to

personal control than we once believed.

6

Small Wonders

Prereading Preparation

Read the passage below. Then answer the questions that follow.

Introduction: Small Wonders

1   When he was nearly three years old, Nguyen Ngoc Truong Son would watch his mother and father playing chess in the family's home in the Mekong Delta and, like any toddler, pester them to let him play, too. Eventually, they relented, assuming the pieces would soon wind up strewn around the kitchen.

5   To his parents' astonishment, Son did not treat the chess set as a plaything. He not only knew how to set up the board, but had also, by careful observation, learned many of the complex rules of the game. Within a month, he was defeating his parents with ease. By age 4, Son was competing in national tournaments against kids many years older. By age 7, he was winning them.

10   Now 12, he is Vietnam's youngest champion and a grand master in the making.

Son's parents are at a loss to explain why their otherwise ordinary child is a whiz at the ancient board game. "It's an inborn gift," says his father, Nguyen Ngoc Sinh. "You couldn't train an ordinary three-year-old to play like that." Son, for his part, doesn't seem to think the question is worth pondering. To him, the nuance-filled strategies and logic of chess play is something that comes as naturally as chewing bubble gum. "I just see things on the board and know what to do," he says matter-of-factly while capturing a *Time* reporter's queen in four moves. "It's just always made sense to me."

15

1. Work with your classmates in small groups. Answer the questions in the chart below, then answer #2.

Nguyen Ngoc Truong Son: A Child Prodigy	
Why is Nguyen Ngoc Truong Son such an unusual child?	
How might you explain his special abilities?	

2. Write a definition of *prodigy*.

   _____

3. Compile the class's answers on the blackboard.

Small Wonders (continued)

by Andrew Marshall
Time Asia

How a child prodigy like Son comes by his preternatural ability is not something that has made much sense to scientists. Only recently has science begun to probe the cultural and biological roots of wunderkinder. New research is showing what scientists have long suspected: that the brains of very smart children appear to function in startlingly different ways from those of average kids. But the question on every parent's mind remains: Are prodigies born, or can prodigies be made? Is giftedness an accident of genetics, or can it be forged through environment—by parents, schools and mentors?

This much is clear: ethnicity and geography are irrelevant. Prodigies can materialize anywhere, and Asia produces more than its share of the superprecocious. In the past, poverty, lack of education and absence of opportunities meant their abilities may have gone undiscovered or undeveloped. But bigger incomes and the rise of an ambitious middle class have produced a boom in accomplished youngsters. A 1997 survey of 32 outstanding physics and chemistry students that was conducted by the National Taiwan Normal University found more than three-quarters of them were the eldest child in small, dual-income households—families with relatively high socioeconomic status. Strictly speaking, however, most of the smart kids in any given home or classroom are not prodigies, no matter how diligent or talented they may be. The standard definition of a prodigy is a child who by age 10 displays a mastery of a field usually undertaken only by adults. "I always say to parents, 'If you have to ask whether your child is a prodigy, then your child isn't one,'" says Ellen Winner, a psychologist in Boston and author of *Gifted Children: Myths and Realities*. Prodigies are, by this definition, exotic creatures whose standout accomplishments are obvious.

Abigail Sin who, at 10 years old, is Singapore's most celebrated young pianist, started reading at age 2, and for the past three years has been ranked among the top 1% in the city-state in an international math competition sponsored by Australia's University of New South Wales. She's smart, but it was only through her music that she qualified as a bona fide prodigy. The youngest Singaporean ever to obtain the coveted Associated Board of the Royal Schools of Music diploma in piano performance, Sin demonstrates one of the hallmark qualities of the breed: a single-minded drive to excel. Winner calls it a "rage to learn," which in Sin's case was manifest in her almost unstoppable urge to master the keyboard since she took her first lesson at age 5. "A lot of kids don't like to sit at the piano for hours," says her tutor Benjamin Loh. "Abigail is different," practicing 25 hours on average a week. "She loves to play, and she learns extraordinarily fast." Her intensity is all the more obvious when she is compared with her twin brother, Josiah, who, like his sister, is good with numbers but doesn't share Abigail's passion for music. "She always practices the same stuff over and over again," he complains.

Where does the drive come from? Researchers are just beginning to understand that there are differences in the functioning of the brain's neural circuitry that appear to differentiate prodigies from their ordinary peers. Neuroscientists have learned more about human gray matter in the past 10 years than in all of previous medical history combined, partly due to the advent of sophisticated technology such as a functional magnetic resonance imaging (fMRI) scanner, which measures blood flow to different segments of the brain, revealing which parts "light up" during various mental activities. The only fMRI scanner in the Southern Hemisphere can be found in Melbourne, where American psychologist Michael O'Boyle has been scanning the brains of young people gifted in mathematics.

He's making some startling discoveries. O'Boyle found that, compared with average kids, children with an aptitude for numbers show six to seven times more metabolic activity in the right side of their brains, an area known to mediate pattern recognition and spatial awareness—key abilities for math and music. Scans also showed heightened activity in the frontal lobes, believed to play a crucial "executive" role in coordinating thought and improving concentration. This region of the brain is virtually inactive in average children when doing the same tasks. Viewed with fMRI, "It's like the difference between a stoplight and a Christmas tree," says O'Boyle, the director of the University of Melbourne's Morgan Center, which researches the development of children who have high intellectual potential. "Not only do math-gifted kids have higher right-side processing power, but this power is also fine-tuned by frontal areas that enhance concentration. These kids are really locked on." O'Boyle believes prodigies also can switch very efficiently between the brain's left and right hemispheres, utilizing other mental resources and perhaps even shutting down areas that produce random distractions. In short, while their brains aren't physically different from ordinary children's, prodigies seem to be able to focus better—to muster the mental resources necessary to solve problems and learn. "For the longest time, these kids' brains were considered the same as everyone else's; they just did twice as much, twice as fast," says O'Boyle. "It turns out those quantitative explanations don't fit. They're doing something qualitatively different." But are prodigies born different, gifted by genetic accident to be mentally more efficient? Or is the management of mental resources something that can be developed? Scientists aren't sure. Studies have shown that raw intelligence, as measured through IQ tests, is highly (though not completely) inheritable. But the connection between high intelligence and prodigious behavior is far from absolute.

With only sketchy evidence to rely on, researchers and other experts continue to debate the age-old "nature vs. nurture" question. "There is no inborn talent for music ability," Schinichi Suzuki, creator of the Suzuki Method of training young musicians, once declared. Even those who believe certain talents are innate agree that a child's upbringing has a big impact on whether a gift is developed or squashed. "Prodigies are half born, half made and mostly discovered at an early age," says Wu Wu-tien, dean of the College of Education at the National Taiwan Normal University. The role adopted by parents is vital. According to psychologist Winner's research, the parents of gifted kids provide stimulating environments: their homes are often full of books; they read to their children at an early age; they take them on trips to museums and concerts. They do not talk down to their children, and they allow them a high degree of independence. And if their child shows talent, they will pull out all the stops to make sure it is encouraged.

Prodigies should not put away childish things simply because they perform as adults, say experts. "Children still need time to be children," says McCann of Flinders University. Violinist Yeou-Cheng Ma—the lesser-known older sister of cellist Yo-Yo—once poignantly remarked of her eight-hours-a-day practice sessions, "I traded my childhood for my good left hand." Even the devoted Singaporean pianist Sin sometimes wants a break from her beloved instrument. "Most of the time I enjoy practicing," she says, "but sometimes I only want to play with Jacky." Jacky is her 18-month-old Yorkshire terrier.

A.

Reading Overview: Main Idea, Details, Summary

Read the passage again. As you read, underline what you think are the most important ideas in the reading. Then, in one or two sentences, write the main idea of the reading. *Use your own words.*

Main Idea

_____

_____

_____

Details

Use the chart below to organize the information in the article. Refer back to the information you underlined in the passage as a guide. When you have finished, write a brief summary of the reading. *Use your own words.*

Small Wonders		
Name of prodigy	1.	2.
How this child excels:		

Question: Are prodigies born or can prodigies be made?			
Organization or Profession	**Name of Spokesperson (If Given)**	**Does this person believe prodigies are born, made, or both?**	**Arguments or Evidence (If Given)**
Author and Psychologist			
Director, University of Melbourne's Morgan Center			
Creator of the Suzuki Method			
National Taiwan Normal University			

Summary

_____

_____

_____

_____

Statement Evaluation

Read the following statements. Then scan the article again quickly to find out if each sentence is **True (T), False (F),** or an **Inference (I).**

1. _____ The biggest difference between child prodigies and average children is the way their brains function.

2. _____ Many child prodigies are Asian.

3. _____ Children with a special aptitude for numbers are always child prodigies.

4. _____ Abigail Sin is a prodigy because of her abilities in math.

5. _____ Josiah Sin is a child prodigy.

6. _____ The brains of very smart children work differently from the way the brains of average children work.

7. _____ Parents are very important in helping gifted children develop their talents.

Reading Analysis

Read each question carefully. Either circle the letter or number of the correct answer or write your answer in the space provided.

1. Read lines 1–7.

    a. What is a **toddler**?

        1. A very smart child
        2. A very young child
        3. A very careful child

    b. What does **astonishment** mean?

        1. Surprise
        2. Satisfaction
        3. Unhappiness

2. Read lines 11–16.

    a. In the sentence, **"Son's parents are at a loss to explain,"** what does **at a loss** mean?

        1. His parents had an explanation for Son's ability, but lost it.
        2. His parents cannot explain Son's special ability.
        3. His parents think that Son has lost his special ability.

    b. What is **the ancient board game**?

        _____

    c. **Pondering** means

        1. thinking about
        2. worrying about
        3. talking about

3. Read lines 19–21.

   a. Which word in this paragraph is a synonym of **child prodigy?**

   _____

   b. What does **probe** mean?
      1. Doubt
      2. Investigate
      3. Understand

4. Read lines 37–39. Define **prodigy**.

   _____

5. Read lines 44–59. Read the sentence, **"Sin demonstrates ... a single-minded drive to excel."** Which two phrases in this paragraph are synonyms of **single-minded drive**?

   _____

6. Read lines 60–62. What does **differentiate** mean?
   a. Distinguish
   b. Remove
   c. Measure

7. Read lines 98–111.

   a. Which word in this paragraph is a synonym for **innate**?

   _____

   b. A child's **upbringing** refers to
      1. the way a child is educated
      2. the way a child is treated
      3. the way a child is taught to behave
      4. all of the above

   c. When parents **pull out all the stops** to encourage their child's talent, they
      1. continuously encourage their child's talent
      2. do everything they possibly can to encourage their child's talent
      3. will not let anyone stop them from encouraging their child's talent

D. DICTIONARY SKILLS

Read the dictionary entry for each word, and consider the context of the sentence from the passage. Write the number of the definition that is appropriate for the context on the line next to the word. Be prepared to explain your choice.

1. To Son, the **nuance**-filled strategies and logic of chess play is something that comes as naturally as chewing bubble gum.

   nuance: _____

   > **nu·ance** \'nü-ˌän(t)s, 'nyü-, -äⁿs; nủ-', nyủ-'\ *n* [F, fr. MF, shade of color, fr. *nuer* to make shades of color, fr. *nue* cloud, fr. L. *nubes;* perh. akin to W *nudd* mist] (1781) **1 :** a subtle distinction or variation **2 :** a subtle quality : NICETY **3 :** sensibility to, awareness of, or ability to express delicate shadings (as of meaning, feeling, or value) — **nu·anced** \-ˌän(t)st, -'än(t)st\ *adj*

2. New research is showing that the brains of very smart children appear to function in startlingly different ways from those of **average** kids.

   average: _____

   > **av·er·age** \'a-v(ə-)rij\ *n* [fr. earlier *average* proportionally distributed charge for damage at sea, modif. of MF *avarie* damage to ship or cargo, fr. OIt *avaria,* fr. Ar *ʻawārī yah* damaged merchandise] (1735) **1 a :** a single value (as a mean, mode, or median) that summarizes or represents the general significance of a set of unequal values **b :** MEAN 1b **2 a :** an estimation of or approximation to an arithmetic mean **b :** a level (as of intelligence) typical of a group, class, or series ⟨above the ~⟩ **3 :** a ratio expressing the average performance esp. of an athletic team or an athlete computed according to the number of opportunities for successful performance — **on average** *or* **on the average :** taking the typical example of the group under consideration ⟨prices have increased *on average* by five

\ə\abut \ᵊ\ kitten, \ər\ further \a\ ash \ā\ ace \ä\ mop, mar \aủ \ out \ch\ chin \e\ bet \ē \ easy \g\go \i\ hit \ī\ ice \j\job \ŋ\sing \ō\ go \ó\ law \ói\ boy \th\ thin \t̲h̲\ the \ü\ loot \ủ\ foot \y\ yet \zh\ vision \á, k̲, ⁿ, œ, œ̄, ʉ, ʉ̄, ʸ\ *See Website below for* Pronunciation Guide.

By permission. From *Merriam-Webster's Online Dictionary* ©2002 by Merriam-Webster, Incorporated (www.Merriam-Webster.com).

3. Sin demonstrates one of the hallmark qualities of the breed: a single-minded **drive** to excel. Ellen Winner calls it a "rage to learn."

   drive: _____

---

drive *n, often attrib* (1785) **1 :** an act of driving: **a :** a trip in a carriage or automobile **b :** a collection and driving together of animals; *also :* the animals gathered **c :** a driving of cattle or sheep overland **d :** a hunt or shoot in which the game is driven within the hunter's range **e :** the guiding of logs downstream to a mill; *also :* the floating logs amassed in a drive **f** (1) : the act or an instance of driving an object of play (as a golf ball) (2) : the flight of a ball **2 a :** a private road : DRIVEWAY **b :** a public road for driving (as in a park) **3 :** the state of being hurried and under pressure **4 a :** a strong systematic group effort ⟨a fund-raising ~⟩ **b :** a sustained offensive effort ⟨the ~ ended in a touchdown⟩ **5 a :** the means of giving motion to a machine or machine part **b :** the means by which the propulsive power of an automobile is applied to the road ⟨front wheel ~⟩ **c :** the means by which the propulsion of an automotive vehicle is controlled and directed ⟨a left-hand ~⟩ **6 :** an offensive, aggressive, or expansionist move; *esp :* a strong military attack against enemy-held terrain **7 a :** an urgent, basic, or instinctual need : a motivating physiological condition of an organism ⟨a sexual ~⟩ **b :** an impelling culturally acquired concern, interest, or longing **c :** dynamic quality **8 :** a device for reading and writing on magnetic media (as tapes or disks)

---

4. Prodigies should not put away childish things simply because they perform as adults, say experts. Violinist Yeou-Cheng Ma once **poignantly** remarked of her eight-hours-a-day practice sessions, "I traded my childhood for my good left hand."

   poignant: _____

---

poi·gnant \'pȯi-nyənt *sometimes* 'pȯi(g)-nənt\ *adj* [ME *poinaunt,* fr. MF *poignant,* prp. of *poindre* to prick, sting, fr. L *pungere* — more at PUNGENT] (14c) **1 :** pungently pervasive ⟨a ~ perfume⟩ **2 a** (1) : painfully affecting the feelings : PIERCING (2) : deeply affecting : TOUCHING **b :** designed to make an impression : CUTTING ⟨~ satire⟩ **3 a :** pleasurably stimulating **b :** being to the point : APT *syn* see PUNGENT, MOVING — **poi·gnant·ly** *adv*

E. Critical Thinking

Read each question carefully. Write your response in the space provided. Remember that there is no one correct answer. Your response depends on what **you** think.

1. According to the author, prodigies can be found anywhere and in any race or culture. What prevents some child prodigies from being discovered or developed? How can these obstacles be overcome so that these children realize their potential?

   _____

   _____

   _____

2. American psychologist Michael O'Boyle found that, "compared with average kids, children with an aptitude for numbers show six to seven times more metabolic activity in the right side of their brains, an area known to mediate pattern recognition and spatial (space) awareness—key abilities for math and music." What do math and music have in common that makes an aptitude for numbers significant?

   _____

   _____

   _____

3. In the nature vs. nurture debate, where do child prodigies stand? Is their special ability due to nature, nurture, or both? Explain your answer.

   _____

   _____

   _____

4. Violinist Yeou-Cheng Ma referring to her eight-hours-a-day practice sessions, said, "I traded my childhood for my good left hand." What did she mean? How do you think she feels about this?

_____

_____

_____

5. Think about your response to #4. Would Abigail Sin agree or disagree with Yeou-Cheng Ma's feelings? Explain your answer.

_____

_____

_____

Another Perspective

Reading at 8 Months? That Was Just the Start

By Michael Winerip

The New York Times

1   Last month, Alia Sabur, a college senior, arrived at her final for Applied Math 301 at 7 P.M. The room was nearly empty. "What were you thinking?" asked her professor, Alan Tucker. The test was actually scheduled from 5 to 7:30 P.M.

5   Alia was thinking, "Time to get started." She sat down and finished in 15 minutes. Afterwards, her mother, Julie, recalls, "She looked very happy. I said, 'Alia, 15 minutes? Did you check it?' Alia said, 'It's fine, Mom.' " And it was. Another perfect score for Alia Sabur. . . .

   Alia, who is 13, and will earn her undergraduate degree from the State
10 University at Stony Brook this spring, has been stunning people for a long time, beginning with her parents, who thought it odd when she started reading words at 8 months old. Prof. Harold Metcalf had her in physics her freshman year. "I was skeptical," he says. "Such a little girl. Then the second or third class, she asked a question. I realized, this girl understands. I've occasionally seen this at
15 15 or 16, but not 10." And not just math and physics. She is also an accomplished clarinetist. . . .

Her professors say that beyond an extraordinary mind, what makes Alia special is a hunger to learn, a willingness to work hard and an emotional balance well beyond her years. This would seem to be every parent's dream, but for a long time it was not. . . . By age 5, Alia had finished the elementary reading curriculum at her Long Island public school. By second grade, she traveled to middle school for eighth-grade math. ("The kids were so big," she recalled).

Things fell apart in the fourth grade. Public school officials said they could no longer accommodate Alia's special needs, Ms. Sabur said, and even Manhattan's best private schools felt she was too advanced. Colleges they consulted would not accept so young a child. . . . Finally, Ms. Sabur got help at Stony Brook. "Their attitude was, 'We're a public university, it's our duty to find a way,' " she said. The mother accompanied the 10-year-old to college every day. She never took notes in lectures—"The concepts are the important part," she said. . . .

Ms. Sabur knows what people think when they hear of her daughter. "They think, 'social misfit,' " she said. Ms. Sabur has worked to help Alia find friends her own age. Twice a week, she schedules an art class and lunch with a group of ninth-grade girls. And while Alia said it felt a little forced at first—"I didn't know a lot of the middle school stuff they were talking about"—she now counts three of the girls as friends. . . . Charles Fortmann, Alia's research adviser, treats her like a colleague. She is helping him with a project on protein folding that could someday lead to a medical breakthrough. . . . He describes Alia as "a quiet person, but you have to listen carefully. If she mentions a problem with something I'm doing, there probably is." Alia is thinking of doing doctoral research next year, attending a music conservatory and performing. . . .

F.

Questions for "Reading at 8 Months? That Was Just the Start."

1. Complete the chart below with Alia's accomplishments and her age at the time.

Accomplishments	Age

2. What are two problems that Alia has had as a result of being a prodigy? Describe the problems and the solutions in the chart below.

Problem:	Problem:

Solution:	Solution:

1. Refer to the **Self-Evaluation of Reading Strategies** on the next page. Think about the strategies you used to help yourself understand "Small Wonders." Check off the strategies you used. Evaluate your strategy use over the first six chapters. Which strategies do you use consistently? Which strategies have you added to the list? Which strategies are becoming automatic? To what extent have you applied these strategies to other reading you do?

2. Child prodigies throughout history, and all over the world, show special talent in many areas: chess, music, and science, for example. Some famous child prodigies are Wolfgang Mozart and Felix Mendelssohn. Search the Internet or go to a library to find out about a child prodigy from another country and/or another time in history. Describe this person's special talent and the kind of life this person has or had.

3. Work with a partner. Choose one of the child prodigies discussed in this chapter. Write a list of questions that you would like to ask this child. Then, trade your list of questions with another pair of students. Have them answer your questions, while you and your partner answer their questions.

SELF-EVALUATION OF READING STRATEGIES

	Readings		
Strategies	"Who Lives Longer?"	"The Mindset of Health"	"Small Wonders"
I read the title and try to predict what the reading will be about.			
I use my knowledge of the world to help me understand the text.			
I read as though I *expect* the text to have meaning.			
I use illustrations to help me understand the text.			
I ask myself questions about the text.			
I use a variety of types of context clues.			
I take chances in order to identify meaning.			
I continue if I am not successful.			
I identify and underline main ideas.			
I connect details with main ideas.			
I summarize the reading in my own words.			
I skip unnecessary words.			
I look up words correctly in the dictionary.			
I connect the reading to other material I have read.			
I do not translate into my native language.			

H. *Topics for Discussion* AND *Writing*

1. In this chapter, many different people give their opinions about the question of whether prodigies are born or made. Whose opinion do you agree with? Why? Explain your answer, and then give your own opinion on this question as well.

2. Some child prodigies as young as 10 years old go to universities. Do you think this is a good environment for these children? Why or why not? Explain your reasons, and give examples to support your opinion.

3. **Write in your journal.** Imagine you discover that your young son or daughter is a child prodigy. What will you do? How will you encourage your child? How will you protect your son or daughter's childhood?

Cloze Quiz

Chapter 6: Small Wonders

Read the passage below. Complete each blank space with one of the words listed. You may use each word only once.

average	drive	inborn	nuance	probe
brains	ethnicity	mathematics	nurture	prodigy
definition	functioning	music	pondering	startlingly
differentiate	giftedness	naturally	previous	wunderkinder

Nguyen Ngoc Truong Son's parents are at a loss to explain why their otherwise ordinary child is a whiz at chess. "It's an _____ gift,"
(1)
says his father. Son doesn't think the question is worth _____.
(2)
To him, the _____ -filled strategies and logic of chess play is
(3)
something that comes as _____ as chewing bubble gum. How
(4)
a child _____ like Son comes by his preternatural ability is not
(5)
something that has made much sense to scientists. Only recently has science
begun to _____ the cultural and biological roots of
(6)
_____. New research is showing that the _____ of
(7)   (8)
very smart children appear to function in _____ different ways
(9)
from the brains of _____ kids. But the question on every
(10)
parent's mind remains: Is _____ an accident of genetics, or can it
(11)
be forged through environment—by parents, schools and mentors?

This much is clear: _____ and geography are irrelevant.
(12)
Prodigies can materialize anywhere.

The standard _____ of a prodigy is a child who by age 10
(13)
displays a mastery of a field usually undertaken only by adults. Abigail Sin

who, at 10 years old, is Singapore's most celebrated young pianist, started reading at age 2. Sin demonstrates one of the hallmark qualities of the breed: a single-minded _____ to excel.
(14)

Where does the drive come from? Researchers are just beginning to understand that there are differences in the _____ of the brain's
(15)
neural circuitry that appear to _____ prodigies from their
(16)
ordinary peers. Neuroscientists have learned more about human gray matter in the past 10 years than in all of _____ medical history
(17)
combined. American psychologist Michael O'Boyle has been scanning the brains of young people gifted in _____.
(18)

With only sketchy evidence to rely on, researchers and other experts continue to debate the age-old "nature vs. _____" question.
(19)
"There is no inborn talent for _____ ability," Shinichi Suzuki,
(20)
creator of the Suzuki Method of training young musicians, once declared.

Unit 2 Review

Crossword Puzzle

Read the clues on the next page. Write the answers in the correct spaces in the puzzle.

Crossword Puzzle Clues

Across

2. When you have a _____, you have a voice in making a decision.
8. An idea, theory, or belief that a person holds
9. An event marking a turning point
10. A _____ element is a vital or crucial element.
11. Inborn; inherited
13. Think about; wonder about
14. Unchangeable
16. The progression through a development of acts or events
18. A _____ is a young child who has just learned to walk (1 to 3 years old).
19. The opposite of **down**
22. Showing good sense
23. The opposite of **no**
24. The past tense of **get**
25. A change from one thing to another
26. When you are a _____, you are an expert at something.
27. The word _____ refers to the heart.

Down

1. Theory
3. An exceptionally bright child
4. The opposite of **subtract**
5. To not eat
6. Examine in depth
7. I want to _____ that. Don't throw it away.
12. Distinguish between two or more things
15. A disadvantage
16. Link
17. A promise to do something
20. All-encompassing; deep
21. The term _____ refers to our environment, to how we are raised.

1. Should parents of child prodigies allow them to go to a university when they are very young? Would it be better for these children to be with others of their own age? Why or why not? What are the **positive aspects** and the **drawbacks** of being a prodigy?

2. Read the questions and then watch the video once or twice. Then answer the questions in groups and discuss them with the whole class.

   A. In what ways is Michael Kearney an ordinary child? In what ways is he extraordinary?

   B. How old was he when he started to read? When do most children start to read? How old were you when you started?

   C. How did Michael feel when he was in college? How was he different from the other students?

   D. Why did Michael's parents have "mixed feelings" about his education?

   E. What did Michael major in? What is he planning to do in Japan? What are his future plans? Do you think he will be successful?

3. Is Michael Kearney's extraordinary intelligence due to **"nature"** or **"nurture"**? What role do you think inheritance has played? What about the way he has been raised by his parents? Has it played an important role?

INFOTRAC® Research Activity

COLLEGE EDITION

The Online Library

Research shows that women generally live longer than men, but is women's longevity due to the fixed factor of gender or to changeable factors? Find articles about the subject by typing in "longevity and women" and "longevity and men" in the InfoTrac College Edition online library. Read the titles of the articles, choose a few that interest you, and read them carefully. What are some reasons that men don't live as long? What behavior changes could help them live as long as women? What types of behavior help women to live longer? Will they continue to live longer, or will men's longevity increase? **Write a journal entry or short report** explaining your findings.

UNIT 3

TECHNOLOGY AND ETHICAL ISSUES

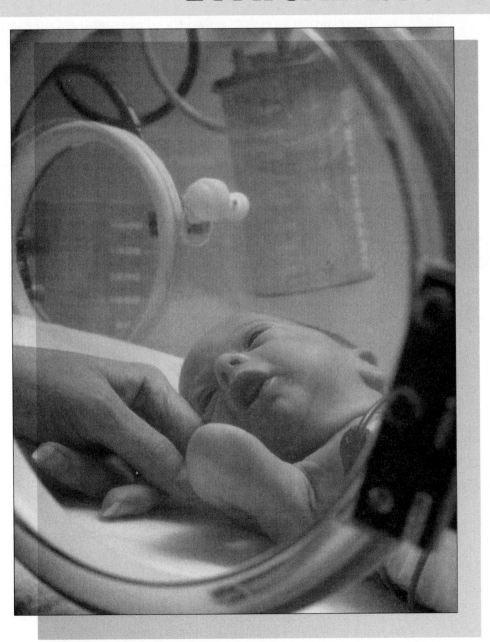

7

Assisted Suicide: Multiple Perspectives

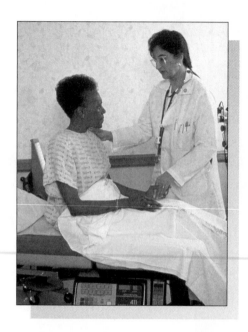

Prereading Preparation

1. This chapter presents a variety of perspectives on assisted suicide. Work with a partner or in a small group. Make a list of the different people who might have different viewpoints on assisted suicide. When you are finished, compare your list with your classmates.

2. Dr. Timothy Quill of the University of Rochester has revealed publicly that he prescribed sleeping pills for Diane, a patient dying of leukemia, knowing that she would use them to end her life. He discussed his decision with *U.S. News's* Amy Bernstein. Below are the questions that she asked him. What do you think were his answers? Work with a partner and discuss what you think he replied. When you are finished, read Dr. Quill's actual answers on the next page and compare them to your own.

Amy Bernstein's Questions

a. How did you make your decision?

_____

_____

b. Have you had second thoughts?

_____

_____

c. Do doctors often assist in suicides?

_____

_____

d. What are the legal consequences?

_____

_____

Dr. Quill's answers:

a. I knew Diane very well and was sure all avenues had been explored. Her alternatives were to tolerate increasing pain and fevers or to be heavily sedated — states worse than death. Sometimes, all one can look forward to is suffering, and our job is to try to lessen that in any way the patient wants. We may not be able to do some things because of personal beliefs, but the goal is to make the patient comfortable—and she defines what that entails, not the doctor.

b. I think about it a lot. I talked to a whole lot of people about it. But I think she got the best care possible.

c. Many doctors have a similar story—a secret about a very personal commitment to a patient that went to the edges of what's accepted.

d. It's a personal, not a legal, matter. This should be debated among clinicians and bioethicists. One purpose of what I did is to have that debate occur with a real case, with a real person who makes a very strong argument. Diane's gone. But there are many Dianes out there.

3. Compare your answers with the answers Dr. Quill gave Ms. Bernstein. Which answers were similar? Which were different?

4. As a member of the medical profession, Dr. Quill offers a particular perspective on assisted suicide. What other perspectives might a doctor have on this issue?

5. Read the following excerpt on the next page from a book written by Dr. Francis Moore. When you finish reading, consider the viewpoints of both Dr. Quill and Dr. Moore. What do each of these doctors consider with regard to the issue of assisted suicide?

Matters of Life and Death (an excerpt)

Dr. Francis Moore
National Academy of Sciences
Joseph Henry Press/National Academy Press

<table>
<tr><td>1</td><td></td></tr>
<tr><td>5</td><td></td></tr>
<tr><td>10</td><td></td></tr>
<tr><td>15</td><td></td></tr>
<tr><td>20</td><td></td></tr>
<tr><td>25</td><td></td></tr>
<tr><td>30</td><td></td></tr>
</table>

In a new book, A Miracle and a Privilege, *Dr. Francis Moore, 81, of Harvard Medical School, discusses a lifetime of grappling with the issue of when to help a patient die. An excerpt:*

Doctors of our generation are not newcomers to this question. Going back to my internship days, I can remember many patients in pain, sometimes in coma or delirious, with late, hopeless cancer. For many of them, we wrote an order for heavy medication—morphine[1] by the clock. This was not talked about openly and little was written about it. It was essential, not controversial.

The best way to bring the problem into focus is to describe two patients whom I cared for. The first, formerly a nurse, had sustained a fractured pelvis in an automobile accident. A few days later her lungs seemed to fill up; her urine stopped; her heart developed dangerous rhythm disturbances. So there she was: in coma, on dialysis, on a breathing machine, her heartbeat maintained with an electrical device. One day after rounds, my secretary said the husband and son of the patient wanted to see me. They told me their wife and mother was obviously going to die; she was a nurse and had told her family that she never wanted this kind of terrible death, being maintained by machines. I told them that while I respected their view, there was nothing intrinsically lethal about her situation. The kidney failure she had was just the kind for which the artificial kidney was most effective. While possibly a bit reassured, they were disappointed. Here was the head surgeon, seemingly determined to keep everybody alive, no matter what.

When patients start to get very sick, they often seem to fall apart all at once. The reverse is also true. Within a few days, the patient's pacemaker could be removed, and she awoke from her coma. About six months later I was again in my office. The door opened and in walked a gloriously fit woman. After some cheery words of appreciation, the father and son asked to speak to me alone. As soon as the door closed, both men became quite tearful. All that came out was, "We want you to know how wrong we were."

The second patient was an 85-year-old lady whose hair caught fire while she was smoking. She arrived with a deep burn; I knew it would surely be fatal. As a remarkable coincidence, there was a seminar going on at the time in medical ethics, given by the wife of an official of our university. She asked me if I had any sort of ethical problem I could bring up for discussion. I described the case and

---

[1]Morphine is a powerful narcotic. It can cause death in large doses (amounts).

asked the students their opinion. After the discussion, I made a remark that was, in retrospect, a serious mistake. I said, "I'll take the word back to the nurses about her, and we will talk about it some more before we decide." The instructor and the students were shocked: "You mean this is a real patient?" The teacher of ethics was not accustomed to being challenged by reality. In any event, I went back and met with the nurses. A day or two later, when she was making no progress and was suffering terribly, we began to back off treatment. When she complained of pain, we gave her plenty of morphine. A great plenty. Soon she died quietly and not in pain. As a reasonable physician, you had better move ahead and do what you would want done for you. And don't discuss it with the world first. There is a lesson here for everybody. Assisting people to leave this life requires strong judgement and long experience to avoid its misuse.

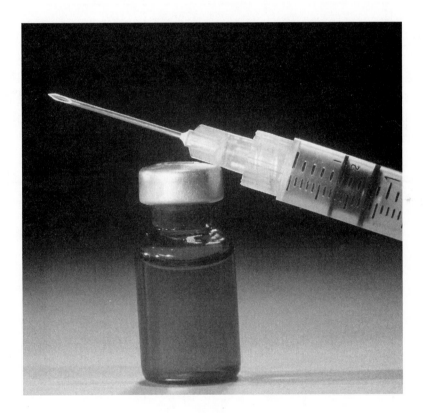

Read the passage again. As you read, underline what you think are the most important ideas in the reading. Then, in one or two sentences, write the main idea of the reading. *Use your own words.*

Main Idea

_____

_____

_____

Details

Use the flowchart on the next page to organize the information in this article. Refer back to the information you underlined in the passage as a guide. When you have finished, write a brief summary of the reading. *Use your own words.*

MATTERS OF LIFE AND DEATH

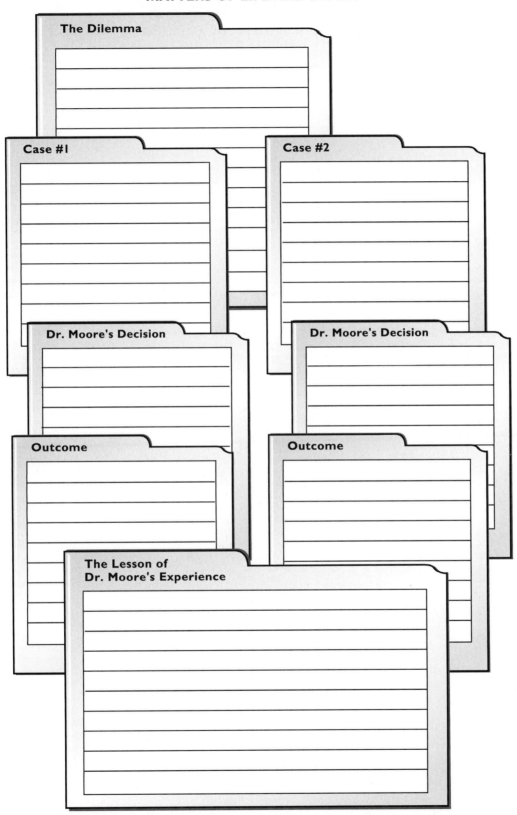

The Dilemma

Case #1

Case #2

Dr. Moore's Decision

Dr. Moore's Decision

Outcome

Outcome

**The Lesson of
Dr. Moore's Experience**

Summary

_____

_____

_____

_____

Statement Evaluation

Read the following statements. Then scan the article again quickly to find out if each sentence is **True (T), False (F),** or an **Inference (I).**

1. _____   The first patient discussed, who was formerly a nurse, died.

2. _____   The first patient's husband and son wanted the doctor to end her life.

3. _____   The instructor and students were very surprised that Dr. Moore was discussing a real patient.

4. _____   Dr. Moore gave the 85-year-old woman enough morphine so that she would die.

5. _____   Dr. Moore would probably choose assisted suicide if he should become terminally ill.

Read each question carefully. Either circle the letter or number of the correct answer or write your answer in the space provided.

1. Read lines 1–6.

    a. An **excerpt** is
        1. an example of an issue
        2. a part of a longer reading
        3. an introduction to a book

    b. **Doctors of our generation** refers to
        1. old doctors
        2. young doctors
        3. doctors about the same age as the author

    c. What does **this question** refer to?

        _____

    d. **My internship days** refers to
        1. the time when the author was younger
        2. a time in the recent past
        3. the time when the author was training as a doctor

2. Read line 7: **"It was essential, not controversial."**

    a. What was essential?

        _____

    b. **Essential** means
        1. necessary
        2. medicine
        3. expensive

    c. **Controversial** refers to
        1. something people agree on
        2. something people argue about
        3. something people have to do

3. Read lines 13–14. **Rounds** refers to

    a. circular motions

    b. when doctors go around a hospital visiting their patients

    c. when a person is put on a breathing machine

4. Read lines 16–17. **"There was nothing intrinsically lethal about her situation"** means
   a. the woman's condition was fatal
   b. the woman's condition was not fatal

5. Read lines 22–25.
   a. What does **"the reverse is also true"** mean?

   _____

   b. Read lines 11–13 and lines 22–25. What is a **pacemaker**?

   _____

   c. How do you know?

   _____

6. Read lines 22–24. Who was **the gloriously fit woman**?

   _____

7. Read lines 29–30. **"I knew it would surely be fatal"** means
   a. the doctor thought the patient might live
   b. the doctor thought the patient might die
   c. the doctor knew the patient would die

8. Read lines 34–39.
   a. **In retrospect** means
      1. looking at something seriously
      2. looking sadly at something
      3. looking back at a past situation
   b. In line 38, **in any event** means
      1. anyway
      2. however
      3. in addition

9. Read lines 43–44. **"Don't discuss it with the world first"** means
   a. don't talk about your patients at seminars
   b. don't talk about your patients with nurses
   c. don't talk to many people about your patients

D. DICTIONARY SKILLS

Read the entry for each word, and consider the context of the sentence from the passage. Write the number of the definition that is appropriate for the context on the line next to the word. **Write the entry number, too, when appropriate.** Be prepared to explain your choice.

1. There was a seminar going on at the time in medical **ethics,** given by the wife of an official of our university.

   ethic: _____

   > **eth·ic** \'e-thik\ *n* [ME, *ethik,* fr. MF *ethique,* fr. L *ethice,* fr. Gk *ēthikē,* fr. *ēthikos*] (14c) **1** *pl but sing or pl in constr* : the discipline dealing with what is good and bad and with moral duty and obligation **2 a :** a set of moral principles or values **b :** a theory or system of moral values ⟨the present-day materialistic ~⟩ **c** *pl but sing or pl in constr* : the principles of conduct governing an individual or a group ⟨professional ~s⟩ **d :** a guiding philosophy

2. The first patient had sustained a **fractured** pelvis in an automobile accident.

   fracture: _____

   > **¹frac·ture** \'frak-chər, -shər\ *n* [ME, fr. L *fractura,* fr. *fractus*] (15c) **1 :** the result of fracturing : BREAK **2 a :** the act or process of breaking or the state of being broken; *esp :* the breaking of hard tissue (as bone) **b :** the rupture (as by tearing) of soft tissue ⟨kidney ~⟩ **3 :** the general appearance of a freshly broken surface of a mineral
   > **²fracture** *vb* **frac·tured; frac·tur·ing** \-chə-riŋ, -shriŋ\ *vt* (1612) **1 a :** to cause a fracture in : BREAK ~a rib **b :** RUPTURE, TEAR **2 a :** to damage or destroy as if by rupturing **b :** to cause great disorder in **c :** to break up : FRACTIONATE **d :** to go beyond the limits of (as rules) : VIOLATE ⟨*fractured* the English language with malaprops — Goodman Ace⟩ ~ *vi :* to undergo fracture

\ə\abut \ᵊ\ kitten, \ər\ further \a\ ash \ā\ ace \ä\ mop, mar \au̇\ out \ch\ chin \e\ bet \ē\ easy \g\go \i\ hit \ī\ ice \j\job \ŋ\sing \ō\ go \ȯ\ law \ȯi\ boy \th\ thin \t͟h\ the \ü\ loot \u̇\ foot \y\ yet \zh\ vision \à, k̲, ⁿ, œ, œ̄, ɯ, ɯ̄ ʸ\ *See Website below for* Pronunciation Guide.

3. The patient's heartbeat was **maintained** with an electrical device
    (a pacemaker).

    The man and his son told me their wife and mother was obviously
    going to die; she had told her family that she never wanted this kind of
    terrible death, being **maintained** by machines.

maintain: _____

main·tain \mān-'tān, mən-\ *vt* [ME *mainteinen,*
fr. OF *maintenir,* fr. ML *manutenēre,* fr. L *manu
tenēre* to hold in the hand] (14c) **1 :** to keep in
an existing state (as of repair, efficiency, or
validity) : preserve from failure or decline
⟨~ machinery⟩ **2 :** to sustain against opposition
or danger : uphold and defend ⟨~ a position⟩
3 : to continue or persevere in : CARRY ON,
KEEP UP ⟨couldn't ~ his composure⟩ **4 a :** to
support or provide for ⟨has a family to ~⟩
b : SUSTAIN ⟨enough food to ~ life⟩ **5 :** to
affirm in or as if in argument ; ASSERT ⟨~*ed* that
the earth is flat⟩ **main·tain·abil·i·ty**
\-ˌtā- nə-'bi-lə-tē\ *n* —**main·tain·able**
\-'tā- nə-bəl\ *adj* **main·tain·er** *n*

syn MAINTAIN, ASSERT, DEFEND, VINDICATE,
JUSTIFY mean to uphold as true, right, just, or
reasonable. MAINTAIN stresses firmness of
conviction ⟨steadfastly *maintained* his
innocence⟩. ASSERT suggests determination to
make others accept one's claim ⟨*asserted* her
rights⟩. DEFEND implies maintaining in the face
of attack or criticism ⟨*defended* his voting
record⟩. VINDICATE implies successfully
defending ⟨his success *vindicated* our faith in
him⟩. JUSTIFY implies showing to be true, just,
or valid by appeal to a standard or to precedent
⟨the action was used to *justify* military
intervention⟩.

4. The first patient had **sustained** a fractured pelvis in an automobile
    accident.

sustain: _____

sus·tain \sə-'stān\ *vt* [ME *sustenen,* fr. OF
sustenir, fr. L *sustinēre* to hold up, sustain, fr.
sub-, sus- up + *tenēre* to hold — more at
SUB-, THIN] (13c) **1 :** to give support or
relief to **2 :** to supply with sustenance :
NOURISH **3 :** KEEP UP, PROLONG **4 :** to
support the weight of : PROP; *also* : to carry
or withstand (a weight or pressure) **5 :** to
buoy up ⟨~*ed* by hope⟩ **6 a :** to bear up
under **b :** SUFFER, UNDERGO ⟨~*ed* heavy
losses⟩ **7 a :** to support as true, legal, or just
b : to allow or admit as valid ⟨the court ~*ed*
the motion⟩ **8 :** to support by adequate
proof : CONFIRM ⟨testimony that ~*s* our
contention⟩ —**sus·tained·ly** \-'stā-nəd-lē,
-'stānd-lē*adv* — **sus·tain·er** *n*

E. *Critical Thinking*

Read each question carefully. Write your response in the space provided. Remember that there is no one correct answer. Your response depends on what **you** think.

1. Reread Dr. Quill's answer to the interviewer's fourth question. Consider his response with regard to Dr. Moore's experience in the medical ethics seminar. Do you think Dr. Moore and Dr. Quill would agree on the matter of debating the ethics of assisted suicide? Explain your answer.

_____

_____

_____

2. What did the husband and the son of the former nurse want the doctor to do? Why were they disappointed?

_____

_____

_____

3. When the father and son revisited him, Dr. Moore states that "both men became quite tearful." Why do you think they reacted this way?

_____

_____

_____

4. Why did the doctors give the 85-year-old woman "plenty of morphine"? What does Dr. Moore mean by **"a great plenty"**?

_____

_____

_____

5. In giving advice, Dr. Moore states, **"And don't discuss it with the world first."** What do you think **"it"** refers to? Why does Dr. Moore say not to discuss it with the world?

_____

_____

_____

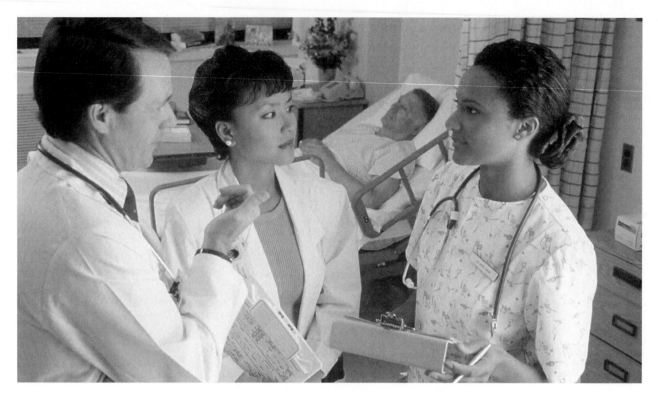

Another Perspective

Should Doctors Be Allowed to Help Terminally Ill Patients Commit Suicide?

by Derek Humphry and Daniel Callahan

Health

YES

1   It would be a great comfort to people who face terminal illness to know they could get help to die if their suffering became unbearable.
5   All pain cannot be controlled, and it's arrogant for anybody to say that it can. Quality of life decisions are the sole right of the individual.

It's nonsense to say that death
10   shouldn't be part of a doctor's job—it already is. We all die. Death is a part of medicine. One of a doctor's jobs is to write death certificates. So this idea of the doctor as superhealer

NO

If it's a question of someone's wanting the right to die, I say jump off a building. But as soon as you bring in somebody else to help you, it changes the equation. Suicide is legally available to people in this country. Just don't ask a doctor to help you do it. That would violate the traditions of medicine and raise doubts about the role of the physician.

One of my worries is that people will be manipulated by a doctor's suggesting suicide. A lot of seriously is a load of nonsense. The fact is that it's not so easy to commit suicide on your own. It's very hard for decent citizens to get deadly drugs. Even if they do, there's the fear that the drugs won't work. There are hundreds of dying people who couldn't lift their hand to their mouth with a cup of coffee, let alone a cup of drugs. They need assistance.

Of course, people who are depressed or who feel they are a weight on their families should be counseled and helped to live. But you have to separate those instances from people who are dying, whose bodies are giving up on them. If you think there is a cure around the corner for your malady, then please wait for it. That is your choice. But sometimes a person realizes that her life is coming to an end, as in the case of my wife, whose doctor said, "There is nothing else we can do."

We're not talking about cases in which a depressed person will come to a doctor and ask to be killed. Under the law the Hemlock Society is trying to get passed, the doctor must say no to depressed people. A candidate for assisted suicide has to be irreversibly, terminally, hopelessly ill and judged to be so by two doctors.

Derek Humphry is the founder of the Hemlock Society and author of Final Exit, *a book advising terminally ill people on how to commit suicide.*

ill people already feel they're a burden because they're costing their families money. It would be easy for a family to insinuate, "While we love you, Grandmother, and we're willing to spend all our money and not send the kids to college, wouldn't it be better if . . . ?" There is no coercion there, but you build on somebody's guilt. We'd have a whole new class of people considering suicide who hadn't thought about it before.

Then, too, I don't believe that you could successfully regulate this practice. The relationship between the doctor and the patient begins in confidentiality. If they decide together that they don't want anybody to know, there is no way the government can regulate it. The presumption is that physicians would only be helping people commit suicide after everything else had failed to end their suffering. But a lot of people won't want to be that far along. None of the proposed regulations takes into account a person who is not suffering now, but who says, "I don't want to suffer in the future. Let me commit suicide now." I can imagine a doctor who would say, "Yes, we're going to make sure that you don't have to suffer at all."

Daniel Callahan is a bioethicist and director of the Hastings Center, a medical ethics think tank in Briarcliff Manor, New York.

1. Describe Derek Humphry's position on doctor-assisted suicide for
   a. terminally ill people

   _____

   _____

   _____

   b. depressed people

   _____

   _____

   _____

2. What do you think happened to Derek Humphry's wife? Why do you think so?

   _____

   _____

   _____

3. Describe Daniel Callahan's position on doctor-assisted suicide for terminally ill people.

   _____

   _____

   _____

4. What are some reasons that Daniel Callahan gives for his opinion?

   _____

   _____

   _____

Follow-up Activities

1. Refer to the **Self-Evaluation of Reading Strategies** on page 206. Think about the strategies you used to help yourself understand "Matters of Life and Death." Check off the strategies you used. Think about the strategies you didn't use, and try to apply them to help yourself understand the readings that follow.

2. Work with one or two classmates. Review the various perspectives given by the authors in this chapter. Whose perspective was included? Whose perspective was omitted? What perspectives might these excluded people have? Make a list of these people and their possible perspectives, and discuss them with the class.

3. a. Work in small groups of three or four students. Discuss the following case.

   "Martin" is a 40-year-old father of two young children. He was recently involved in a serious car accident and was critically injured. The doctors have declared him "brain dead," which means that his brain does not show any mental activity at all. He is being kept alive on a feeding tube and a respirator that breathes for him because he cannot breathe on his own. The doctors do not believe he will ever improve. However, he could be kept alive, but unconscious, on the machines indefinitely. The family must make an extremely difficult decision: Should they continue to keep Martin on these machines in the hospital, which is costing thousands of dollars a day, or should they allow him to die? Although Martin's family does not have a lot of money, they love him very much. What do you think they should do? What might be the consequences of the decision you think they should make?

   b. Form a medical ethics committee. Discuss all the class groups' decisions and their possible consequences. Then, as a class, decide what you think Martin's family should do.

   c. Think about how you came to your decision. What factors or values influenced your decision?

H. Topics for Discussion AND Writing

1. In the United States, some people write a "living will" before their death. A "living will" can prevent doctors from prolonging a person's life if he or she becomes seriously ill. For example, this means that the person may not want to be resuscitated if he or she stops breathing, or placed on a respirator or feeding tube if he or she cannot breathe or eat on his or her own. Would you want to write a "living will"? If not, why not? If so, under what conditions would you want to be allowed to die naturally? Write a composition explaining your answer.

2. What is your opinion on doctor-assisted suicide? Should it be legal? Should it be banned? Write a paragraph stating your opinion. Then discuss your opinion with your classmates.

3. **Write in your journal.** If someone you loved were terminally ill and wanted his or her doctor to perform an assisted suicide, would you approve? Would you encourage the doctor to agree to assist in the suicide? Explain your reasons.

Cloze Quiz

Chapter 7: Assisted Suicide: Multiple Perspectives—Matters of Life and Death

Read the passage below. Fill in the blanks with one word from the list. Use each word only once.

awoke	ethics	internship	medication	sick
case	fatal	lethal	problem	smoking
describe	fractured	machines	reality	students
essential	in retrospect	maintained	respected	their

Doctors of our generation are not newcomers to this question. Going back to my _____ days, I can remember many patients in pain,
(1)

sometimes in coma, with late, hopeless cancer. For many of them, we wrote an order for heavy _____—morphine by the clock. This was not
(2)

talked about openly, and little was written about it. It was _____,
(3)

not controversial.

The best way to bring the problem into focus is to _____
(4)

two patients whom I cared for. The first, formerly a nurse, had sustained a

_____ pelvis in an automobile accident. A few days later her
(5)

lungs seemed to fill up; her heart developed dangerous rhythm disturbances.

So there she was: in coma, on a breathing machine, her heartbeat

_____ with an electrical device. One day the husband and son
(6)

of the patient came to see me. They told me _____ wife and
(7)

mother was obviously going to die; she had told her family that she never

wanted this kind of terrible death, being maintained by _____.
(8)

I told them that while I _____ their view, there was nothing
(9)

intrinsically _____ about her situation. While possibly a bit
(10)
reassured, they were disappointed.

When patients start to get very _____, they often seem to
(11)
fall apart all at once. The reverse is also true. Within a few days, the patient's
pacemaker could be removed and she _____ from her coma.
(12)

The second patient was an 85-year-old lady whose hair caught fire while
she was _____. She arrived with a deep burn; I knew it would
(13)
surely be _____. As a remarkable coincidence, there was a
(14)
seminar going on at the time in medical _____, given by the
(15)
wife of an official of our university. She asked me if I had any sort of ethical
_____ I could bring up for discussion. I described the
(16)
_____ and asked the students their opinion. After the
(17)
discussion, I made a remark that was, _____, a serious mistake. I
(18)
said, "I'll take the word back to the nurses about her, and we will talk about it
some more before we decide." The instructor and the _____
(19)
were shocked: "You mean this is a real patient?" The teacher of ethics was
not accustomed to being challenged by _____.
(20)

CHAPTER

8

Sales of Kidneys Prompt New Laws and Debate

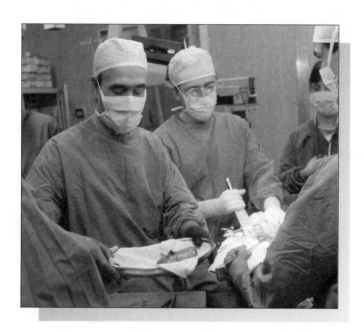

Prereading Preparation

Read the following article. Then complete the survey and answer the questions that follow.

Trading Flesh Around the Globe

Time

1   A ghoulish[1] notion: people so poor that they sell some of their body parts to survive. But for scores of brokers who buy and sell human organs in Asia, Latin America and Europe, that theme from a late-night horror movie is merely a matter of supply and demand. There are thousands more patients in need of
5   kidneys, corneas, skin grafts and other human tissue than there are donors; therefore, big money can be made on a thriving black market in human flesh.

In India, the going rate for a kidney from a live donor is $1,500; for a cornea, $4,000; for a patch of skin, $50. Two centers of the thriving kidney trade are

---

[1]*Ghoulish* is the adjective form of *ghoul*, which refers to a legendary evil creature that robs graves and eats the dead. It is an extremely negative word.

Bombay, where private clinics cater to Indians and a foreign clientele dominated
by wealthy Arabs, and Madras, a center for patients from Malaysia, Singapore
and Thailand. Renal patients in India and Pakistan who cannot find a relative to
donate a kidney are permitted to buy newspaper advertisements offering living
donors up to $4,300 for the organ. Mohammad Aqeel, a poor Karachi tailor who
recently sold one of his kidneys for $2,600, said he needed the money "for the
marriage of two daughters and paying off of debts."

In India, Africa, Latin America, and Eastern Europe, young people advertise
organs for sale, sometimes to pay for college educations. In Hong Kong a
businessman named Tsui Fung circulated a letter to doctors in March offering to
serve as middleman between patients seeking the kidney transplants and a
Chinese military hospital in Nanjing that performs the operation. The letter said
the kidneys would come from live "volunteers," implying that they would be
paid donors. The fee for the kidney, the operation and round-trip airfare:
$12,800.

1. Work with your classmates in small groups. Answer the following survey about selling
    organs. When you are finished, compile the class's answers on the blackboard.

Would you sell:	Student 1	Student 2	Student 3	Student 4
one of your kidneys?	Yes/No	Yes/No	Yes/No	Yes/No
one of your corneas?	Yes/No	Yes/No	Yes/No	Yes/No
a patch of your skin?	Yes/No	Yes/No	Yes/No	Yes/No
a lobe from your lung?	Yes/No	Yes/No	Yes/No	Yes/No

2. Look at the results of your class survey. What are the conditions under which your
    classmates would sell their organs? Ask the students who answered *yes* to complete the
    following statement:

    I would sell _____ for the following reasons: _____
    _____.

3. Read the title of this article. What new laws and what debate do you think the sale of
    kidneys has prompted?

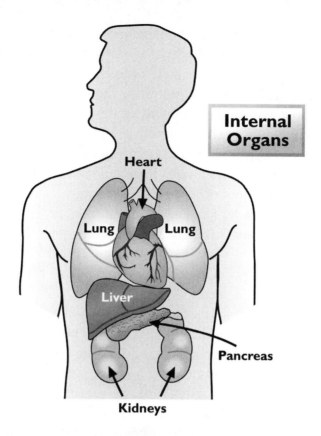

Internal Organs

Heart

Lung   Lung

Liver

Pancreas

Kidneys

Sales of Kidneys Prompt New Laws and Debate

by Terry Trucco
The New York Times

1   Last summer Colin Benton died after receiving a kidney transplant at a private London hospital. Several months later, however, his case made headlines throughout Britain when his widow disclosed that her husband's kidney transplant had come from a Turkish citizen who was paid $3,300 to fly to Britain
5   and donate the organ. The donor said he had decided to sell his kidney to pay for medical treatment for his daughter. Concern in Britain over issues raised in the case resulted in a law passed on July 28, 1989, in Parliament banning the sale of human organs for transplant.

The same concerns and those over loopholes in the transplant laws in some
10   other nations led the World Health Organization to condemn the practice recently. In a resolution in May, the organization asked member nations to take appropriate measures, including legislation, to prohibit trafficking in human organs.

But as Britain was moving to make the sale of human organs unlawful, as it
15   is in the United States, ethicists and policy analysts in the United States were

beginning to suggest that paying donors, or their estates, may be an effective way to increase the supply of organs available for transplant.

The idea of organs for sale "is creeping into health care discussions," Joel L. Swerdlow said in a recent report for the Annenberg Washington Program, a public policy research group affiliated with Northwestern University in Evanston, Illinois. "The altruistic 'gift relationship' may be inadequate as a motivator and an anachronism in medicine today," he wrote. "If paying seems wrong, it may nevertheless be preferable to accepting the suffering and death of patients who cannot otherwise obtain transplants."

Doctors, lawyers and health authorities say the sale of organs by impoverished donors is a growing phenomenon. Because it is possible to live with just one kidney and because demand for the organs is so high, kidneys are among the most popular organs for commercial transactions. People have sold their own blood for years.

The new British law makes it a criminal offense to give or receive money for supplying organs of either a living or dead person. It also prohibits acting as a broker in such an arrangement, advertising for organs for payment or transplanting an organ from a live donor not closely related to the recipient.

A new computerized nationwide registry, which records all transplants from both live donors and cadavers, will be used to help enforce the law. Punishment for breaking the law is either a $3,300 fine or three months in prison. Doctors convicted under the law could lose their right to practice medicine.

The health organization's resolution calls for compiling information on organ trafficking laws in member countries and publicizing the findings. At least 20 other countries, including the United States, Canada and most of Western Europe, already have laws or policies prohibiting the sale of human organs.

Britain has had a transplant law since the 1961 Human Tissue Act, which deemed it unethical for a practitioner to traffic in human organs. But the new law is believed to be the world's first legislation aimed exclusively at the commercial organ transactions. The British law applies only to transplants performed in the nation's private hospitals and not to those overseen by the government-supported National Health Service, which provides free medical care for British citizens. The service, which has not used paid donors, gets first pick of all kidneys available for transplant in the nation. At present, about 1,600 transplants are performed each year, with a waiting list of about 3,600 patients.

But, as in the United States, many patients from countries without high-quality kidney care come to Britain each year to undergo transplants in private hospitals. These hospitals rely on cadaver kidneys or live donor transplants from relatives of patients.

In the past, doctors simply questioned foreign donors to make certain they were related to recipients, but most admit the system was hardly foolproof. Often doctors could not communicate with patients who did not speak English. A doctor involved in the Benton case said he attempted to find out if the donor had been paid by waving a 5-pound note at him. "A number of us were duped by patients with forged medical referrals and documents saying they were relatives," said Maurice Slapak, director of a hospital transplant unit in Britain.

Despite the speed and ease with which the British transplant law was passed, it remains controversial. In a letter to *The Times* of London, Royden Harrison, professor emeritus at Warwick University, wrote: "What possible objection can there be if one person, of their own free will, should sell their kidney to someone else? The seller is able to indulge in a few of the good things in life. The buyer may well be paying to survive." Sir Michael McNair Wilson, a member of Parliament who is on a waiting list for a new kidney, has argued that selling a kidney is like women in the nineteenth century selling their hair. "As someone waiting to receive a transplant, I would only like to feel that the organ I am given is a gift from someone," he said. "But while there is a shortage of kidneys, I do not see why it is wrong for you to do what you will with your body."

"If it takes $25,000 to $30,000 annually to keep someone alive on an artificial kidney machine," John M. Newman wrote in the Annenberg Program report, "government payment of, for example, $5,000 for transplantable cadaver kidneys (even with the cost of transportation), would still make successful kidney transplantation cost effective." Dr. Newman, a kidney transplant recipient, is a director of the American Association of Kidney Patients. "This is not to suggest that a monetary value can be placed on human life or on life-saving organs," he added. "This does suggest, however, that a monetary 'thank you' from the Federal Government could stimulate increases in organ and tissue availability for transplantation and research."

There is concern that the new law could scare off suitable donors and add to the shortage of kidneys by somehow creating the impression that all donations are improper. A report by the National Kidney Research Fund said there had been a dramatic fall in the number of kidney donations earlier this year following the kidney-for-sale controversy. "There have effectively been at least 100 fewer transplant operations this year, and that means 100 people may have died because of the unfavorable publicity," the organization said in a statement.

Some opponents of the law simply think that it is addressing the wrong health issue. Elizabeth Ward, founder of the British Kidney Patients Association, supports legislation that would make organ donation automatic upon death. Those who choose not to donate would have to make a formal request. But Belgium began such a program several years ago, and it has had little effect. Doctors are reluctant to use the law. Doctors still ask next of kin for permission to remove organs. It's a moral issue. Nevertheless, many in the medical profession think the law was needed.

100   "If we take the very extreme view, people in desperate circumstances might be prepared to martyr themselves, selling their hearts to save their families," said Ross Taylor, director of transplant surgery at the Royal Victoria Infirmary in Newcastle Upon Tyne and president of the British Transplantation Society. Mr. Taylor also criticized those tempted to sell their organs for frivolous reasons. "I

105   have met people prepared to sell their kidneys to buy Porsches or to take a girlfriend on a holiday."

Read the passage again. As you read, underline what you think are the most important ideas in the reading. Then, in one or two sentences, write the main idea of the reading. *Use your own words.*

Main Idea

_____

_____

_____

Details

Use the outline on the next page to organize the information in the article. Refer back to the information you underlined in the passage as a guide. When you have finished, write a brief summary of the reading. *Use your own words.*

SALES OF KIDNEYS PROMPT NEW LAWS AND DEBATE

	Britain	World Health Organization	United States	Belgium
Laws about organ donation				
Opinions about sales of organs				⨉
Arguments in favor of a law prohibiting the sale of organs	1. 2. 3.			
Arguments against a law prohibiting the sale of organs	1. 2. 3.			

Summary

_____

_____

_____

_____

Read the following statements. Then scan the article again quickly to find out if each sentence is **True (T), False (F),** or **Not Mentioned (NM)** in the article.

1. _____ In Britain it is legal to sell organs.

2. _____ The World Health Organization supports the sale of organs for transplants.

3. _____ In the United States it is unlawful to sell organs.

4. _____ Some policy analysts in the United States think that paying donors may increase the number of organ transplants.

5. _____ Most of Asia already has laws prohibiting the sale of human organs.

6. _____ In Britain organ donation is automatic when someone dies.

7. _____ Dr. John M. Newman paid the person who donated a kidney to him.

8. _____ In Belgium organ donation is automatic when someone dies.

Read each question carefully. Either circle the letter or number of the correct answer or write your answer in the space provided.

1. Read lines 1–8 in *Sales of Kidneys*.
    a. Who is the **donor**?
        1. The person who receives the organ
        2. The person who gives the organ
    b. In the sentence **"Concern in Britain over issues raised in the case ... ,"** what is one of the **issues** in this **case**?
        1. Colin Benton's kidney donor was paid $3,300.
        2. Colin Benton died after his kidney transplant.

2. Read lines 9–13.
    a. What does **the practice** refer to?

    _____

    b. **To prohibit trafficking in human organs** means
        1. to allow the buying and selling of human organs
        2. to forbid the buying and selling of human organs
        3. to control the buying and selling of human organs

3. Read lines 25–26. **Impoverished donors** are
    a. healthy
    b. important
    c. poor

4. Read lines 50–51.
    a. In **"The service ... gets first pick ... ,"** what is **the service**?

    _____

    b. **"Gets first pick"** means the service
        1. has first choice of the available kidneys
        2. can decide which hospital gets kidneys

5. Read lines 55–56.
   a. What are **live donors** and **cadavers**?
      1. Opposites
      2. Synonyms
   b. What is a **cadaver**?
      1. A donor
      2. An organ
      3. A dead body

6. Read lines 75–79. **"$5,000 for transplantable cadaver kidneys . . . would still make successful kidney transplantation cost effective"** means
   a. it's less expensive to pay a donor for a kidney than it is to keep someone alive on an artificial kidney machine
   b. it's less expensive to keep someone alive on an artificial kidney machine than it is to pay a donor for a kidney

7. Read lines 97–98. Who are **next of kin**?
   a. Lawyers
   b. Other doctors
   c. Family members

8. Read lines 100–106.
   a. What does **to martyr themselves** mean?
      1. To die
      2. To undergo an operation
      3. To put themselves in danger
   b. What are examples of **frivolous reasons** why people might sell their organs?

   _____

   c. What does **frivolous** mean?
      1. Exciting; fun
      2. Minor; trivial
      3. Expensive; costly

D. DICTIONARY SKILLS

Read the entry for each word and consider the context of the sentence from the passage. Write the definition that is appropriate for the context in the line next to the word. **Write the entry number, too, when appropriate.** Be prepared to explain your choice.

1. Some opponents of the British transplant law think that it **addresses** the wrong health issue.

   address: _____

   > **ad·dress** \ə-'dres, a- *also* 'a-ˌdres\ *vb* [ME
   > *adressen,* fr. MF *adresser,* fr. *a-* (fr. L *ad-*) +
   > *dresser* to arrange — more at DRESS] *vt* (14c)
   > **1** *archaic* **a :** DIRECT, AIM **b :** to direct to
   > go : SEND **2 a :** to direct the efforts or
   > attention of (oneself) ⟨will ~ himself to the
   > problem⟩ **b :** to deal with : TREAT
   > ⟨intrigued by the chance to ~ important issues
   > — I. L. Horowitz⟩ **3** *archaic :* to make
   > ready; *esp :* DRESS **4 a :** to communicate
   > directly ⟨~*es* his thanks to his host⟩ **b :** to
   > speak or write directly to; *esp :* to deliver a
   > formal speech to **5 a :** to mark directions
   > for delivery on ⟨~ a letter⟩ **b :** to consign to
   > the care of another (as an agent or factor)
   > **6 :** to greet by a prescribed form **7 :** to
   > adjust the club preparatory to hitting (a golf
   > ball) **8 :** to identify (as a peripheral or
   > memory location) by an address or a name
   > for information transfer ~ *vi, obs :* to direct
   > one's speech or attentions — **ad·dress·er** *n*

\ə\abut \ə\ kitten, \ər\ further \a\ ash \ā\ ace \ä\ mop, mar \aᴜ\ out \ch\ chin \e\ bet \ē\ easy \g\go \i\ hit \ī\ ice \j\job \ŋ\sing \ō\ go \ȯ\ law \ȯi\ boy \th\ thin \t͟h\ the \ü\ loot \u̇\ foot \y\ yet \zh\ vision \à, k̟, ⁿ, œ, œ̄, ᵫ, ᵫ̄ ʸ\ *See Website below for* Pronunciation Guide.

By permission. From *Merriam-Webster's Online Dictionary* ©2002 by Merriam-Webster, Incorporated (www.Merriam-Webster.com).

2. Colin Benton's case made headlines when his widow **disclosed** that his kidney transplant had come from a Turkish citizen.

   disclose: _____

   > **dis·close** \dis-'klōz\ *vt* [ME, fr. MF *desclos-,* stem of *desclore* to disclose, fr. ML *disclaudere* to open, fr. L *dis-* + *claudere* to close — more at CLOSE] (14c) **1** *obs* : to open up **2 a :** to expose to view **b** *archaic* : HATCH **c :** to make known or public ⟨demands that politicians ~ the sources of their income⟩ *syn* see REVEAL — **dis·close·er** *n*

3. a. The World Health Organization recently condemned the **practice** of selling human organs for transplant.

   b. Doctors who are convicted under the British transplant law may lose their medical license and their **practice.**

   practice: (a) _____ (b) _____

   > **practice** *also* **practise** *n* (15c) **1 a :** actual performance or application ⟨ready to carry out in ~ what they advocated in principle⟩ **b :** a repeated or customary action ⟨had this irritating ~⟩ **c :** the usual way of doing something ⟨local ~s⟩ **d :** the form, manner, and order of conducting legal suits and prosecutions **2 a :** systematic exercise for proficiency ⟨~ makes perfect⟩ **b :** the condition of being proficient through systematic exercise ⟨get in ~⟩ **3 a :** the continuous exercise of a profession **b :** a professional business; *esp* : one constituting an incorporeal property *syn* see HABIT

By permission. From *Merriam-Webster's Online Dictionary* ©2002 by Merriam-Webster, Incorporated (www.Merriam-Webster.com).

4. The World Health Organization wants member nations to create legislation that would make it illegal to **traffic in** human organs. In fact, Britain's transplant law deems it unethical for a practitioner to **traffic in** any human organs.

traffic in: _____

---

¹traf·fic \'tra-fik\ *n, often attrib* [MF *trafique,* fr. OIt *traffico,* fr. *trafficare* to traffic] (1506) **1 a :** import and export trade **b :** the business of bartering or buying and selling **c :** illegal or disreputable usu. commercial activity ⟨the drug ~⟩ **2 a :** communication or dealings esp. between individuals or groups **b :** EXCHANGE ⟨a lively ~ in ideas — F. L. Allen⟩ **3** *archaic* : WARES, GOODS **4 a :** the movement (as of vehicles or pedestrians) through an area or along a route **b :** the vehicles, pedestrians, ships, or planes moving along a route **c :** the information or signals transmitted over a communications system : MESSAGES **5 a :** the passengers or cargo carried by a transportation system **b :** the business of transporting passengers or freight **6 :** the volume of customers visiting a business establishment *syn* see BUSINESS — **the traffic will bear :** existing conditions will allow or permit ⟨charge what *the traffic will bear*⟩
²traffic *vb* **traf·ficked; traf·fick·ing** *vi* (1540) : to carry on traffic ~ *vt* **1 :** to travel over ⟨heavily *trafficked* highways⟩ **2 :** TRADE, BARTER — **traf·fick·er** *n*

E. Critical Thinking

Read each question carefully. Write your response in the space provided. Remember that there is no one correct answer. Your response depends on what **you** think.

1. Does the author present the information in the article subjectively or objectively? Explain the reasons for your answer.

   _____

   _____

2. How do you think Terry Trucco, the journalist who wrote the kidney sales article, feels about this issue? What makes you think this?

   _____

   _____

3. Refer to the case of Colin Benton.
   a. Why did Mrs. Benton's disclosure make headlines throughout Britain?

      _____

      _____

   b. What issues do you think were raised as a result of this case?

      _____

      _____

4. Compare the growing attitude in the United States to the new legislation in Britain. How are the policies of the two countries changing?

   _____

   _____

5. Both Sir Michael McNair Wilson and Dr. John M. Newman are in favor of the sale of human organs for transplants. What do you think might be some reasons for their opinion?

   _____

   _____

   _____

6. Sir Michael McNair Wilson has argued that selling a kidney is like women in the nineteenth century selling their hair. Do you think this is a reasonable comparison? Explain your answer.

_____

_____

_____

7. Elizabeth Ward suggests that organ donation should be made automatic upon death unless the individual specifically requests otherwise. Why does she think this is a better approach to the issue of organ donations than Britain's new law is?

_____

_____

_____

F.   Follow-up Activities

1. Refer to the **Self-Evaluation of Reading Strategies** on page 206. Think about the strategies you used to help yourself understand "Sales of Kidneys Prompt New Laws and Debate." Check off the strategies you used. Think about the strategies you didn't use, and try to apply them to help yourself understand the readings that follow.

2. Look at the following chart carefully, then answer the related questions.

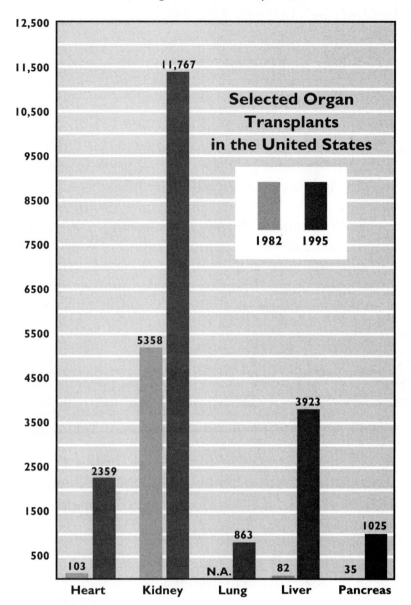

Selected Organ Transplants in the United States

1982   1995

Heart: 103, 2359
Kidney: 5358, 11,767
Lung: N.A., 863
Liver: 82, 3923
Pancreas: 35, 1025

a. What does this graph compare?

_____

b. 1. In 1982, what type of organ transplant was most frequent?

_____

2. In 1995, what type of organ transplant was most frequent?

_____

3. Based on what you read in the article, what is the reason this organ is transplanted most frequently?

_____

c. 1. Which organ transplant operation increased the most in absolute numbers between 1982 and 1995?

_____

2. Which organ transplant operation showed the highest percentage of increase between 1982 and 1995?

_____

3. a. Below is a list of nine people who need heart transplants. Working alone, place these people in order of priority for a transplant. What factors (e.g., age, sex) should determine which patients receive priority?

b. Work in a group of three or four students. Your group is a panel of medical experts at a leading hospital in a large city. Your group must decide on the order in which to place these patients on the list to receive an organ. Discuss your individual decisions, then negotiate a single list of people in the order they will be placed on the waiting list.

Your Order	Your Group's Order	Sex	Age	Occupation	Personal Information	Length of Time Already Waiting
		F	36	housewife	3 children	12 months
		M	6	first grader	—	18 months
		M	71	heart surgeon	2 children, 3 grandchildren	9 months
		M	40	truck driver	widowed, 1 child	9 months
		F	24	kindergarten teacher	single, 2 siblings	12 months
		F	15	high school student	5 siblings	18 months
		F	47	cancer specialist	divorced, no children	12 months
		F	39	ESL teacher	married, 3 children	6 months
		M	52	banker	married, 1 child	10 months

UNIT **3**   Technology and Ethical Issues

G. Topics for Discussion AND Writing

1. In the United States, it is illegal to sell or buy organs. Do you think that governments have the right or the responsibility to make laws controlling the sale of organs? What are your reasons? Should this be a legal issue or a moral issue? Do you think it is wrong to buy or sell organs? Why or why not? Discuss your opinion with your classmates.

2. In Belgium, when a person dies, his or her organs are automatically donated unless that person had formally requested not to donate before he or she died. Do you think this is a good program? Would you want to donate your organs after your death? Why or why not? Write a paragraph explaining your answer.

3. Do you think the sale of organs from live donors will continue to be considered a moral issue, or will people come to see their nonvital organs as "investments" to be sold in time of economic need? If they do, does the government have the right to prevent people from selling their organs? Why or why not? If an individual wants to sell an organ in order to make money, does a surgeon have the right and/or the responsibility to refuse to perform the operation? Write a composition explaining your opinions.

4. Look back at the organ transplant chart on page 183. What do you think may be some reasons for the great increase in transplants in general? Discuss these reasons with your classmates.

5. **Write in your journal.** Would you volunteer as a living organ donor? If so, under what circumstances would you do so? If not, why not?

Chapter 8: Sales of Kidneys Prompt New Laws and Debate

Read the passage below. Fill in the blanks with one word from the list. Use each word only once.

banning	disclosed	law	practice	supply
cadaver	hospitals	organ	punishment	traffic
countries	impoverished	pick	recipient	transplant
dead	kidneys	possible	sale	waiting

Last summer Colin Benton died after receiving a kidney

_____ at a private London hospital. Several months later,
(1)

however, his case made headlines throughout Britain when his widow

_____ that her husband's kidney transplant had come from a
(2)

Turkish citizen who was paid $3,300 to fly to Britain and donate the

_____. Concern in Britain over issues raised in the case resulted
(3)

in a law passed on July 28, 1989, in Parliament _____ the sale of
(4)

human organs for transplant.

But as Britain was moving to make the _____ of human
(5)

organs unlawful, as it is in the United States, ethicists and policy analysts in

the United States were beginning to suggest that paying donors, or their

estates, may be an effective way to increase the _____ of organs
(6)

available for transplant.

Doctors, lawyers and health authorities say the sale of organs by

_____ donors is a growing phenomenon. Because it is
(7)

_____ to live with just one kidney and because demand for the
(8)

organs is so high, _____ are among the most popular organs for
                              (9)
commercial transactions.

The new British _____ makes it a criminal offense to give or
                           (10)
receive money for supplying organs of either a living or _____
                                                                    (11)
person. It also prohibits acting as a broker in such an arrangement,
advertising for organs for payment or transplanting an organ from a live
donor not closely related to the _____.
                                          (12)
A new computerized nationwide registry, which records all transplants
from both live donors and cadavers, will be used to help enforce the law.
_____ for breaking the law is either a $3,300 fine or three
        (13)
months in prison. Doctors convicted under the law could lose their right to
_____ medicine.
        (14)
Britain has had a transplant law since the 1961 Human Tissue Act, which
deemed it unethical for a practitioner to _____ in human
                                                    (15)
organs. The British law applies only to transplants performed in the nation's
private _____ and not to those overseen by the government-
              (16)
supported National Health Service, which provides free medical care for
British citizens. The service, which has not used paid donors, gets first
_____ of all kidneys available for transplant in the nation. At
        (17)
present, about 1,600 transplants are performed each year, with a
_____ list of about 3,600 patients.
        (18)
But, as in the United States, many patients from _____
                                                              (19)
without high-quality kidney care come to Britain each year to undergo
transplants in private hospitals. These hospitals rely on _____
                                                                    (20)
kidneys or live donor transplants from relatives of patients.

The Gift of Life: When One Body Can Save Another

Prereading Preparation

1. Read the title of this article. Discuss it with a classmate. What do you think this reading will be about?

2. Read the following paragraphs about organ transplants. Then work with a partner to answer the questions.

Paragraph One

A doctor's new dilemma: two weeks ago, Ronald Busuttil, director of UCLA's liver-transplant program, heard that a liver, just the right size and blood type, was suddenly available for a man who had been waiting for a transplant. The patient, severely ill but not on the verge of death, was being readied for the procedure when the phone rang. A 5-year-old girl who had previously been given a transplant had suffered a catastrophe. Her liver had stopped functioning. Busuttil had to make a decision. "I had two desperately ill patients," he says, but the choice was clear. Without an immediate transplant, "the little girl certainly would have died."

    a. What was the doctor's dilemma?

_____

b. Describe each patient's condition:

The man's: _____

The little girl's: _____

c. What did the doctor decide to do?

_____

_____

d. Do you agree with his decision? Why or why not?

_____

_____

Paragraph Two

   In the world of advanced medical technology, the uses of living tissue have become very suddenly more complex and problematic. A newly born infant suffering from the fatal congenital malformation known as anencephaly will surely die within a few days of birth. Anencephaly means a partial or complete absence of the cerebrum, cerebellum and flat bones of the skull. Such babies could be an invaluable source for organs and tissues for other needy infants. Is that sort of "harvesting" all right?

a. Is an anencephalic infant healthy? Why or why not?

_____

b. What will happen to such an infant?

_____

c. What is the ethical dilemma in this case?

_____

d. What is your opinion on this matter? In other words, *"Is that sort of 'harvesting' all right?"*

_____

The Gift of Life: When One Body Can Save Another

by Lance Morrow
Time

1 Now the long quest was ending. A 14-month-old girl named Marissa Ayala lay anesthetized upon an operating table in the City of Hope National Medical Center in Duarte, Calif. A surgeon inserted a one-inch-long needle into the baby's hip and slowly began to draw marrow. In 20 minutes, they removed about
5 a cup of the viscous red liquid.

The medical team then rushed the marrow to a hospital room where Marissa's 19-year-old sister Anissa lay waiting. Through a Hickman catheter inserted in the chest, the doctor began feeding the baby's marrow into Anissa's veins. The marrow needed only to be dripped into the girl's bloodstream. There
10 the healthy marrow cells began to find their way to the bones.

Done. If all goes well, if rejection does not occur or a major infection set in, the marrow will do the work. It will give life to the older sister, who otherwise would have died of chronic myelogenous leukemia. Doctors rate the chance of success at 70%.

15 The Ayala family had launched itself upon a sequence of nervy, life-or-death adventures to arrive at the denouement last week. Anissa's leukemia was diagnosed three years ago. In such cases, the patient usually dies within five years unless she receives a marrow transplant. Abe and Mary Ayala, who own a speedometer-repair business, began a nationwide search for a donor whose
20 marrow would be a close match for Anissa's. The search, surrounded by much poignant publicity, failed.

The Ayalas did not passively accept their daughter's fate. They knew from their doctors that the best hope for Anissa lay in a marrow transplant from a sibling, but the marrow of her only brother, Airon, was incompatible. Her life, it
25 seemed, could depend on a sibling who did not yet exist.

First, Abe had to have his vasectomy surgically reversed, a procedure with a success rate of just 40%. That done, Mary Ayala ventured to become pregnant at the age of 43. The odds were one in four that the baby's bone marrow would match her sister's. In April 1990 Mary bore a daughter, Marissa. Fetal stem cells
30 were extracted from the umbilical cord and frozen for use along with the marrow in last week's transplant. Then everyone waited for the optimum moment—the baby had to grow old enough and strong enough to donate safely even while her older sister's time was waning.

Twelve days before operation, Anissa began receiving intensive doses of
35 radiation and chemotherapy to kill her diseased bone marrow. As a result, she is losing her hair. Her blood count is plummeting. Her immune system has gone

out of business. But in two to four weeks, the new cells should take over and start their work of giving Anissa a new life.

    The drama of the Ayalas—making the baby, against such long odds, to save the older daughter—seemed to many to be a miracle. To others, it was profoundly, if sometimes obscurely, troubling. What disturbed was the spectacle of a baby being brought in to the world . . . to serve as a means, a biological resupply vehicle. The baby did not consent to be used. The parents created the new life then used that life for their own purposes, however noble. Would the baby have agreed to the transplant if she had been able to make the choice?

    People wanting a baby have many reasons—reasons frivolous, sentimental, practical, emotional, biological. Farm families need children to work the fields. In much of the world, children are social security for old age. They are vanity items for many people, an extension of ego. Or a sometimes desperate measure to try to save a marriage that is failing. Says Dr. Rudolf Brutoco, Marissa Ayala's pediatrician: "Does it make sense to conceive a child so that little Johnny can have a sister, while it is not acceptable to conceive the same child so that Johnny can live?" In American society, procreation is a personal matter. Crack addicts or convicted child abusers are free to have children.

    Considered on the family's own terms, their behavior is hard to fault. The first duty of parents is to protect their children. The Ayalas say they never considered aborting the fetus if its marrow did not match Anissa's. They will cherish both daughters in the context of a miracle that allowed the older to live on and the younger to be born.

    But their case resonated with meanings and dilemmas larger than itself. The case opened out upon a prospect of medical-technological possibility and danger. In the past it was mostly cadavers from which transplant organs were "harvested." Today, as with the Ayalas, life is being tapped to save life.[1]

    Beyond the Ayala case, the ethics can become trickier. What if a couple conceives a baby in order to obtain matching marrow for another child; and what if amniocentesis shows that the tissue of the fetus is not compatible for transplant? Does the couple abort the fetus and then try again? Says Dr. Norman Fost, a pediatrician and ethicist at the University of Wisconsin: "If you believe that a woman is entitled to terminate a pregnancy for any reason at all, then it doesn't seem to me to make it any worse to terminate a pregnancy for this reason." But abortions are normally performed to end accidental pregnancies. What is the morality of ending a pregnancy that was very deliberately undertaken in the first place?

[1]Postscript: The transplant operation was successful. Anissa survived and Marissa suffered no adverse effects from the procedure.

Transplant technology is developing so rapidly that new practices are outpacing society's ability to explore their moral implications. The first kidney transplants were performed over 35 years ago and were greeted as the brave new world: an amazing novelty. Today the transplant is part of the culture— conceptually dazzling, familiar in a weird way, but morally unassimilated. The number of organ transplants exceeds 15,000 a year and is growing at an annual clip of 15%. The variety of procedures is also expanding as surgeons experiment with transplanting parts of the pancreas, the lung and other organs. As of last week, 23,276 people were on the waiting list of the United Network for Organ Sharing, a national registry and tracking service.

A dire shortage of organs for these patients helps make the world of transplants an inherently bizarre one. Seat-belt and motorcycle-helmet laws are bad news for those waiting for a donor. The laws reduce fatalities and therefore reduce available cadavers.

Most organs come from cadavers, but the number of living donors is rising. There were 1,778 last year, up 15% from 1989. Of these, 1,773 provided kidneys, nine provided portions of livers. Six of the living donors gave their hearts away. How? They were patients who needed heart-lung transplant packages. To make way for the new heart, they gave up the old one; doctors call it the "domino practice."

In 1972 Dr. Thomas Starzl, the renowned Pittsburgh surgeon who pioneered liver transplants, stopped performing live-donor transplants of any kind. He explained why in a speech in 1987: "The death of a single well-motivated and completely healthy living donor almost stops the clock worldwide. The most compelling argument against living donation is that it is not completely safe for the donor." Starzl said he knew of 20 donors who had died, though other doctors regard this number as miraculously low, since there have been more that 100,000 live-donor transplants.

There will never be enough cadaver organs to fill the growing needs of people dying from organ or tissue failure. This places higher and higher importance, and risk, on living relatives who might serve as donors. Organs that are either redundant (one of a pair of kidneys) or regenerative (bone marrow) become more and more attractive. Transplants become a matter of high-stakes risk calculation for the donor as well as the recipient and the intense emotions involved sometimes have people playing long shots.

Federal law now prohibits any compensation for organs in the United States. In China and India, there is a brisk trade in such organs as kidneys. Will the day come when Americans have a similar marketplace for organs? Turning the body into a commodity might in fact make families less willing to donate organs.

Reading Overview: Main Idea, Details, and Summary

Read the passage again. As you read, underline what you think are the most important ideas in the reading. Then, in one or two sentences, write the main idea of the reading. *Use your own words.*

Main Idea

_____

_____

_____

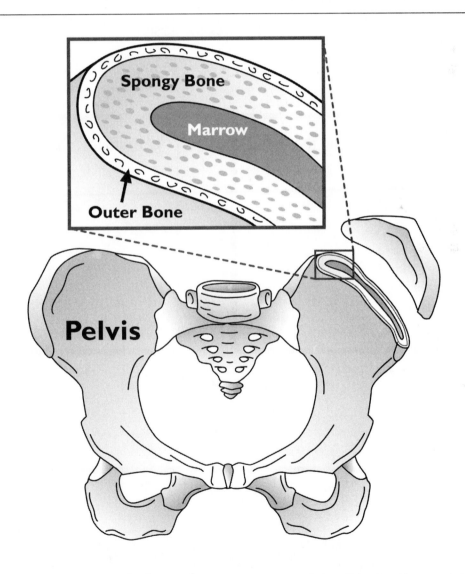

Details

Use the flowchart below to organize the information in the reading. Refer back to the information you underlined in the passage as a guide. When you have finished, write a brief summary of the reading. *Use your own words.*

THE GIFT OF LIFE: WHEN ONE BODY CAN SAVE ANOTHER

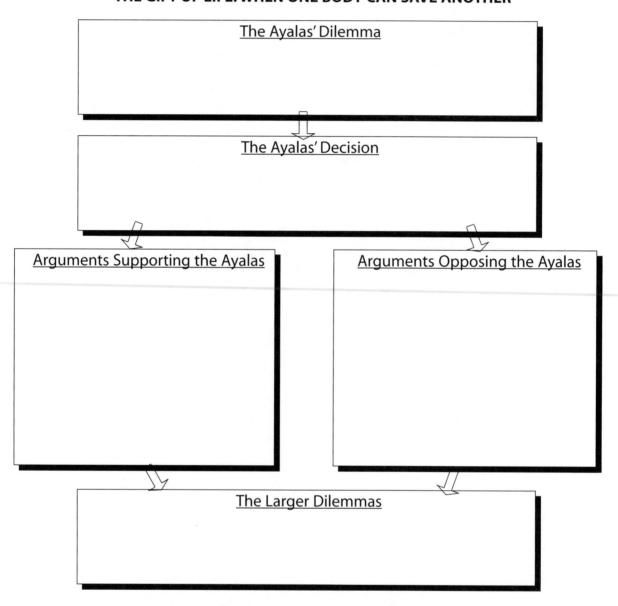

The Ayalas' Dilemma

The Ayalas' Decision

Arguments Supporting the Ayalas

Arguments Opposing the Ayalas

The Larger Dilemmas

Summary

_____

_____

_____

_____

B. Statement Evaluation

Read the following statements. Then scan the article again quickly to find out if each sentence is **True (T)**, **False (F)**, or an **Inference (I)**.

1. _____   The bone marrow was taken from 19-year-old Anissa and given to 14-month-old Marissa.

2. _____   The older sister has a very serious disease.

3. _____   Marissa was born before Anissa became sick with leukemia.

4. _____   Dr. Rudolf Brutoco agreed with the Ayalas' decision to conceive a child in the hopes of saving Anissa.

5. _____   Dr. Norman Fost believes that the ethics of terminating a pregnancy is the same no matter what the reason.

6. _____   Living donors have given their hearts away.

7. _____   Dr. Thomas Starzl worries that an organ recipient may die as a result of the transplant operation.

Read each question carefully. Either circle the letter or number of the correct answer, or write your answer in the space provided.

1. Read lines 6–9. A **catheter** is
   a. a type of medicine
   b. a thin plastic tube
   c. a small hole

2. Read lines 11–12. **"If all goes well"** means
   a. if the procedure works correctly
   b. if the sister dies
   c. if rejection occurs

3. Read lines 15–18.
   a. **Denouement** means
      1. problem
      2. solution
      3. hospital
   b. What does **in such cases** refer to?

   _____

4. Read lines 22–25.
   a. What was **their daughter's fate**?
      1. She would be sick for a long time.
      2. She would die within five years.
      3. She would receive marrow from a stranger.
   b. **"The marrow of her only brother . . . was incompatible"** means
      1. the marrow of Airon and Anissa was the same
      2. the marrow of Airon and Anissa was different
   c. **A sibling who did not yet exist** is a sibling who
      1. has not been conceived yet
      2. has already been born
      3. is not yet old enough

5. Read lines 31–33.

    a. When is the **optimum moment**?

    _____

    _____

    b. **Optimum** means

        1. best
        2. worst
        3. after one year

6. Read lines 43–45. In this paragraph, what word is a synonym of **consent**?

    _____

7. Read lines 53–54. What is **procreation**?

    a. Having children
    b. Taking drugs
    c. Making a choice

8. Read lines 67–71. To have an **abortion** means to

    a. become pregnant
    b. terminate a pregnancy
    c. continue a pregnancy

9. Read lines 84–87.

    a. What are **seat-belt and motorcycle-helmet laws**?

    _____

    b. Why are these laws **"bad news for those waiting for a donor"**?

    _____

    _____

10. Read lines 96–101.

    a. **"The death of a . . . completely healthy living donor almost stops the clock worldwide"** means that the death of a healthy living donor

        1. discourages other healthy people from donating an organ
        2. discourages doctors from performing transplant operations using healthy living donors
        3. both 1 and 2

    b. **Compelling** means

       1. convincing
       2. healthy
       3. interesting

11. Read lines 109–111. **Prohibits any compensation** means

    a. you cannot receive money for donating an organ
    b. you cannot donate an organ from a cadaver
    c. you cannot donate an organ from a living donor

D. DICTIONARY SKILLS

Read the entry for each word and consider the context of the sentence from the passage. Write the definition that is appropriate for the context on the line next to the word. **Write the entry number, too, when appropriate.** Be prepared to explain your choice.

1. There will never be enough cadaver organs to fill the growing needs of people dying from organ or tissue **failure.**

   failure: _____

   > **fail·ure** \ˈfā(ə)l-yər\ *n* [alter. of earlier *failer*, fr. AF, fr. OF *faillir* to fail] (1643)
   > **1 a :** omission of occurrence or performance; *specif* : a failing to perform a duty or expected action **b :** a state of inability to perform a normal function ⟨kidney ~⟩ — compare HEART FAILURE **c :** a fracturing or giving way under stress ⟨structural ~⟩ **2 a :** lack of success **b :** a failing in business : BANKRUPTCY **3 a :** a falling short : DEFICIENCY ⟨a crop ~⟩ **b :** DETERIORATION, DECAY **4 :** one that has failed

2. Considered on the family's own terms, the Ayalas' behavior (conceiving a baby to save their daughter) is hard to **fault.**

   fault: _____

   > **fault** *vi* (15c) **1 :** to commit a fault : ERR **2 :** to fracture so as to produce a geologic fault ~ *vt* **1 :** to find a fault in ⟨easy to praise this book and to ~ it — H. G. Roepke⟩ **2 :** to produce a geologic fault in **3 :** BLAME, CENSURE ⟨can't ~ them for not coming⟩

\ə\abut \ᵊ\ kitten, \ər\ further \a\ ash \ā\ ace \ä\ mop, mar \au̇\ out \ch\ chin \e\ bet \ē \ easy \g\go \i\ hit \ī\ ice \j\job \ŋ\sing \ō\ go \ȯ\ law \ȯi\ boy \th\ thin \th̲\ the \ü\ loot \u̇\ foot \y\ yet \zh\ vision \à, k̲, ⁿ, œ, œ̄, ue, ūe, ʸ\ *See Website below for* Pronunciation Guide.

By permission. From *Merriam-Webster's Online Dictionary* ©2002 by Merriam-Webster, Incorporated (www.Merriam-Webster.com).

3. In 1972 Dr. Thomas Starzl, the renowned Pittsburgh surgeon who **pioneered** liver transplants, stopped performing live-donor transplants of any kind.

pioneer: _____

> **¹pi·o·neer** \ˌpī-ə-'nir\ *n* [MF *pionier,* fr. OF *peonier* foot soldier, fr. *peon* foot soldier, fr. ML *pedon-, pedo* — more at PAWN] (1523) **1 :** a member of a military unit usu. of construction engineers **2 a :** a person or group that originates or helps open up a new line of thought or activity or a new method or technical development **b :** one of the first to settle in a territory **3 :** a plant or animal capable of establishing itself in a bare, barren, or open area and initiating an ecological cycle
>
> **²pioneer** *vi* (1780) : to act as a pioneer ⟨~*ed* in the development of airplanes⟩ ~ *vt* **1 :** to open or prepare for others to follow; *also* : SETTLE **2 :** to originate or take part in the development of
>
> **³pioneer** *adj* (1840) **1 :** ORIGINAL, EARLIEST **2 :** relating to or being a pioneer; *esp* : of, relating to, or characteristic of early settlers or their time

4. The drama of the Ayalas—making the baby, against such long odds, to save the older daughter—seemed to many to be a miracle. To others, it was **profoundly,** if sometimes obscurely, troubling.

profound: _____

> **pro·found** \prə-'faund, prō-\ *adj* [ME, fr. MF *profond* deep, fr. L. *profundus,* fr. *pro-* before + *fundus* bottom — more at PRO-, BOTTOM] (14c) **1 a :** having intellectual depth and insight **b :** difficult to fathom or understand **2 a :** extending far below the surface **b :** coming from, reaching to, or situated at a depth : DEEP-SEATED ⟨a ~ sigh⟩ **3 a :** characterized by intensity of feeling or quality **b :** all encompassing : COMPLETE ⟨~ sleep⟩ — **pro·found·ly** \-'faun(d)-lē\ *adv* — **pro·found·ness** \-'faun(d)-nəs\ *n*

By permission. From *Merriam-Webster's Online Dictionary* ©2002 by Merriam-Webster, Incorporated (www.Merriam-Webster.com).

E. *Critical Thinking*

Read each question carefully. Write your response in the space provided. Remember that there is no one correct answer. Your response depends on what **you** think.

1. What do you think is Dr. Rudolf Brutoco's opinion of the Ayalas' decision to have another child in the hopes of saving their daughter's life?

    _____

    _____

    _____

2. a. Why did Dr. Starzl stop performing live-donor transplants of any kind?

    _____

    _____

    b. Why do other doctors regard the number of donors who have died as "miraculously low"?

    _____

    _____

3. Why will there be a "higher and higher importance, and risk" for living relatives who may become donors?

    _____

    _____

    _____

Another Perspective

Two Parents Offer Their Daughter the Breath of Life—to No Avail

Time

1   Did Cindy and Roger Plum of Coon Rapids, Minnesota, overstep the limits of parental sacrifice to try to save their 9-year-old daughter Alyssa? Although their efforts failed, both parents say they would do it again—and again.

5   Last New Year's Eve, Alyssa took to bed with symptoms that suggested bronchitis. Three months later, she was rushed to a hospital emergency room with a high fever. Doctors suspected a virus, but sent her home. Two days later, Alyssa was at her doctor's office with pneumonia. Within days, her skin turned blue from lack of oxygen. By mid-April she was on a list for a lung transplant.

The Plums, who had read about transplant surgeries using lobes of the lung
10   from living donors, decided to volunteer. Alyssa successfully received a piece of Roger's lung. Then her other lung failed. Less than four weeks later, Cindy underwent the procedure. This time Alyssa died of heart failure. Both parents have 18-inch scars that run from their chest to their back. Cindy's sleep is still interrupted by pain. Roger suffers from muscle weakness. Even though the
15   couple have a son, Travis, 6, who risked losing a parent, they never had doubts about their actions. "If I didn't give Alyssa a chance at life," says Cindy, "I didn't know if I could live with myself."

1. a. How many lung lobe transplants did Alyssa receive?

   _____

   b. Were they successful?

   _____

2. Why did 6-year-old Travis risk losing a parent?

   _____

   _____

3. a. What adverse effects do Cindy and Roger Plum suffer from the transplants?

   _____

   _____

   b. Do the Plums have any regrets about the transplants?

   _____

Follow-up Activities

1. Refer to the **Self-Evaluation of Reading Strategies** on the next page. Think about the strategies you used to help yourself understand "The Gift of Life." Check off the strategies you used. Evaluate your strategy use over the first nine chapters. Which strategies have you begun to use that you didn't use before? Which strategies do you use consistently? Which strategies have you added to the list? Which strategies are becoming automatic? To what extent have you applied these strategies to other reading you do?

SELF-EVALUATION OF READING STRATEGIES

Strategies	Readings		
	"Matters of Life and Death"	"Sales of Kidneys"	"The Gift of Life"
I read the title and try to predict what the reading will be about.			
I use my knowledge of the world to help me understand the text.			
I read as though I *expect* the text to have meaning.			
I use illustrations to help me understand the text.			
I ask myself questions about the text.			
I use a variety of types of context clues.			
I take chances in order to identify meaning.			
I continue if I am not successful.			
I identify and underline main ideas.			
I connect details with main ideas.			
I summarize the reading in my own words.			
I skip unnecessary words.			
I look up words correctly in the dictionary.			
I connect the reading to other material I have read.			
I do not translate into my native language.			

2. Conduct an in-class survey using the questions in the following chart. Record the responses on the chart. (You may use your data later if you decide to do an out-of-class survey on the same questions.) Discuss the responses in class.

Questions	Yes	No
1. Is it morally acceptable for parents to conceive a child in order to obtain an organ or tissue to save the life of another one of their children?		
2. Is it morally acceptable to remove a kidney or other nonessential organ from a living person for use in another person's body?		
3. Would you donate a kidney for transplant to a close relative who needed it?		
4. Is it ethical to ask a child under the age of 18 to give up a kidney for a transplant to a relative?		
5. If you or a close relative had a fatal disease that could possibly be cured by a transplant, which of these would you be willing to do? a. Purchase the necessary organ or tissue b. Conceive a child to provide the necessary organ or tissue c. Take legal action to force a relative to donate		

H. Topics for Discussion AND Writing

1. In a recent magazine survey, 47% of American people said that they believe it is acceptable for parents to conceive a child in order to obtain an organ or tissue to save the life of another one of their children. However, 37% of American people believe that this would be unacceptable. What do you think? Write a letter to the magazine in support of or against this idea. Be sure to make your reasons clear.

2. In your country, what do you think is the general opinion on living-to-living organ donation (for example, a kidney or a lung lobe)? Is this practice legal? Write a paragraph about this type of organ donation in your country. When you are finished, compare it with your classmates' descriptions of organ donation in their countries. How are the policies similar in various countries? How are they different?

3. **Write in your journal.** What is your opinion about the Ayala case? Do you approve of their decision to have another child in order to save their older daughter? Explain your opinion.

Cloze Quiz

Chapter 9: The Gift of Life: When One Body Can Save Another

Read the passage below. Fill in the blanks with one word from the list. Use each word only once.

consent	failed	life	radiation	success
denouement	frivolous	marrow	rejection	surgeon
disturbed	incompatible	optimum	safely	transplant
donor	launched	pregnant	sibling	unless

A 14-month-old girl named Marissa Ayala lay anesthetized upon an operating table in the City of Hope National Medical Center. A

_____ inserted a one-inch-long needle into the baby's hip and
(1)

slowly began to draw marrow.

The medical team then rushed the _____ to a hospital room
(2)

where Marissa's 19-year-old sister Anissa lay waiting. The doctor fed the

baby's marrow into Anissa's veins. There the healthy marrow cells began to

find their way to the bones.

Done. If all goes well, if _____ does not occur or a major
(3)

infection set in, the marrow will do the work. It will give life to the older sister,

who otherwise would have died of leukemia. Doctors rate the chance of

success at 70%.

The Ayala family had _____ itself upon a sequence of nervy,
(4)

life-or-death adventures to arrive at the _____ last week.
(5)

Anissa's leukemia was diagnosed three years ago. In such cases, the patient

usually dies within five years _____ she receives a marrow
(6)

transplant. Abe and Mary Ayala, began a nationwide search for a

_____ whose marrow would be a close match for Anissa's. The
          (7)
search _____ .
          (8)

The Ayalas did not passively accept their daughter's fate. They knew

from their doctors that the best hope for Anissa lay in a marrow transplant

from a _____ , but the marrow of her only brother, Airon, was
          (9)

_____ . Her life, it seemed, could depend on a sibling who did
          (10)
not yet exist.

First, Abe had to have his vasectomy surgically reversed, a procedure

with a _____ rate of just 40%. That done, Mary Ayala ventured to
          (11)
become _____ at the age of 43. In April 1990 Mary bore a
          (12)
daughter, Marissa. Then everyone waited for the _____
                                                          (13)
moment—the baby had to grow old enough and strong enough to donate

_____ , even while her older sister's time was waning.
          (14)
Twelve days before operation, Anissa began receiving intensive doses of

_____ and chemotherapy to kill her diseased bone marrow. But
          (15)
in two to four weeks, the new cells should take over and start their work of

giving Anissa a new life.

The drama of the Ayalas—making the baby, against such long odds, to

save the older daughter—seemed to many to be a miracle. To others, it was

profoundly, if sometimes obscurely, troubling. What _____ was
                                                              (16)
the spectacle of a baby being brought in to the world . . . to serve as a means,

a biological resupply vehicle. The baby did not _____ to be
                                                          (17)
used. The parents created the new _____ , then used that life for
                                          (18)
their own purposes, however noble. Would the baby have agreed to the

_____ if she had been able to make the choice?
          (19)
People wanting a baby have many reasons—reasons _____ ,
                                                              (20)
sentimental, practical, emotional, biological. Farm families need children to

work the fields. In much of the world, children are social security for old age.

They are vanity items for many people, an extension of ego.

Unit 3 Review

J. Crossword Puzzle

Read the clues on the next page. Write the answers in the correct spaces in the puzzle.

Crossword Puzzle Clues

Across

2. This paragraph is part of a longer reading. It is an _____ from a reading.

6. The past tense of **put**

7. An electronic device that controls the heartbeat

10. The _____ time to do something is the best time to do it.

14. Deadly; terminal

17. Topics such as capital punishment, euthanasia, and assisted suicide are very _____.

18. Kidneys, heart, lungs, pancreas, liver

20. The solution to a problem or a difficult situation is its _____.

22. Very poor

23. A _____ is a person who sacrifices himself for a cause or for another person.

25. Looking in _____ means looking back at a past event.

26. Make known; reveal

Down

1. The opposite of **down**

3. A thin plastic tube used in medical procedures

4. When we _____ something to be right or wrong, we judge it to be right or wrong.

5. Minor; trivial

8. Necessary

9. A person who gives something voluntarily is a _____.

11. The center part of bone

12. Keep in an existing state

13. A dead body; a corpse

15. A subject of investigation

16. Reflex; involuntary

19. Direct one's efforts or attention to

21. A code of _____ is a system of moral values.

24. I, me; we, _____

1. Ben and Mary Ayala conceived a child in the hope that she would be a suitable donor of bone marrow for her sister, who had leukemia. Do you think the Ayalas were right to have a baby for this reason? Why or why not?

2. Read the statements below and then watch the video once or twice. Decide whether each sentence is **True (T), False (F),** or **Not Mentioned (NM).**

   A. _____ The Ayalas were both over 40 when they decided to try to have another child, Marissa.

   B. _____ The odds were 1 out of 4 that Marissa's marrow would be a close match for Anissa's.

   C. _____ Marissa would have given her consent for the bone marrow transplant if she had been able to.

   D. _____ The type of leukemia Anissa had is not usually fatal.

   E. _____ Most patients who have Anissa's form of leukemia survive the transplant operation.

3. What kinds of ethical issues does the case of the Ayala sisters involve? Should couples be prohibited from having babies to harvest their marrow or organs? Should organs or marrow be removed from a patient without the patient's consent? Is parental consent sufficient?

In recent years, there has been controversy regarding people selling their kidneys and other organs. Find articles on this subject by typing "kidneys for sale" and "human organs for sale" into the InfoTrac College Edition online library.

What are the positive and negative sides of the practice of selling organs? Find some arguments that support the sale of organs. Why do some people believe the sale of organs should be allowed? Should donors be compensated? How should they be paid? Do most people who sell their organs do so for frivolous reasons, or do they really need the money? Why do some people oppose the sale of these organs? How big a problem is the illegal sale of organs from cadavers? Should trafficking in human organs be prohibited?

Take one side and argue your opinion in a composition, or organize a debate between partners or groups. Provide examples from the online readings.

UNIT 4

THE ENVIRONMENT

10

Playing with Fire

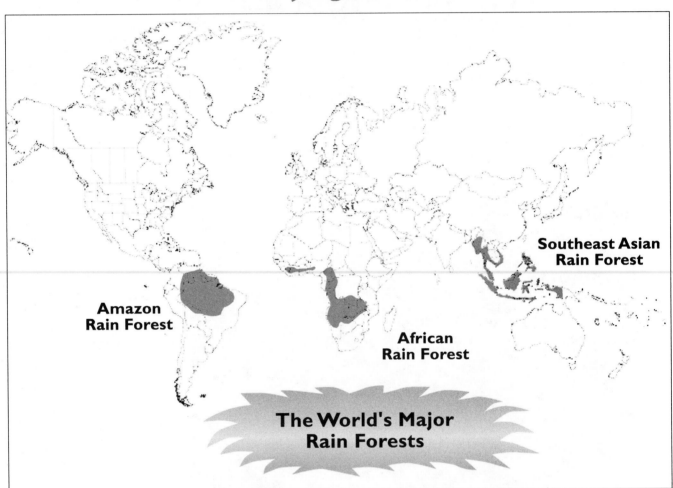

Amazon
Rain Forest

African
Rain Forest

Southeast Asian
Rain Forest

The World's Major
Rain Forests

Prereading Preparation

1. The title "Playing with Fire" has a double meaning. In other words, it has two meanings: a literal meaning and a figurative meaning.

    a.   What is the literal meaning of "Playing with Fire"?

    b.   What is the figurative meaning of "Playing with Fire"?

2. What is a rain forest? Where are rain forests located?

3. The rain forests of the Amazon are being destroyed. The following questions will be discussed in this article. Work with a partner. Write down any answers that you may have to these questions. After you have finished the article, check and complete your answers.

Questions	Answers
1. Who or what is destroying the rain forests?	
2. How are the rain forests being destroyed?	
3. Why are the rain forests being destroyed?	
4. How can rain forests be important to people?	
5. How can rain forests be important to the environment?	

Playing with Fire

by Laura Lopen, *Rio de Janeiro,* John Maier, *Porto Velho,* and Dick Thompson, *Washington*
Time

1   The skies over western Brazil will soon be dark both day and night. Dark from the smoke of thousands of fires, as farmers and cattle ranchers engage in their annual rite of destruction: clearing land for crops and livestock by burning the rain forests of the Amazon. Unusually heavy rains have slowed down the
5   burning this year, but the dry season could come at any time, and then the fires will reach a peak. Last year the smoke grew so thick that Porto Velho, the capital of the state of Rondonia, was forced to close its airport for days at a time. An estimated 12,250 square miles of Brazilian rain forest—an area larger than Belgium—was reduced to ashes. . . .
10   After years of inattention, the whole world has awakened at last to how much is at stake in the Amazon. It has become the front line in the battle to rescue earth's endangered environment from humanity's destructive ways. "Save the rain forest," long a rallying cry for conservationists, is now being heard from

politicians, pundits and rock stars. The movement has sparked a confrontation between rich industrial nations, which are fresh converts to the environmental cause, and the poorer nations of the Third World, which view outside interference as an assault on their sovereignty. . . .

The vast region of unbroken green that surrounds the Amazon River and its tributaries has been under assault by settlers and developers for 400 years. Time and again, the forest has defied predictions that it was doomed. But now the danger is more real and imminent than ever before as loggers level trees, dams flood vast tracts of land and gold miners poison rivers with mercury. In Peru the forests are being cleared to grow coca for cocaine production. "It's dangerous to say the forest will disappear by a particular year," says Philip Fearnside of Brazil's National Institute for Research in the Amazon, "but unless things change, the forest *will* disappear."

That would be more than a South American disaster. It would be an incalculable catastrophe for the entire planet. Moist tropical forests are distinguished by their canopies of interlocking leaves and branches that shelter creatures below from sun and wind, and by their incredible variety of animal and plant life. If the forests vanish, so will more than one million species—a significant part of the earth's biological diversity and genetic heritage. Moreover, the burning of the Amazon could have dramatic effects on global weather patterns—for example, heightening the warming trend that may result from the greenhouse effect. . . .

The river and forest system covers 2.7 million square miles (almost 90% of the area of the contiguous United States) and stretches into eight countries besides Brazil. . . . The jungle is so dense and teeming that all the biologists on earth could not fully describe its life forms. A 1982 U.S. National Academy of Sciences report estimated that a typical four-square mile patch of rain forest may contain 750 species of trees, 125 kinds of mammals, 400 types of birds, 100 sorts of reptiles and 60 types of amphibians. Each type of tree may support more than 400 insect species. . . .

But the diversity of the Amazon is more than just good material for TV specials. The rain forest is a virtually untapped storehouse of evolutionary achievement that will prove increasingly valuable to mankind as it yields its secrets. Agronomists see the forest as a cornucopia of undiscovered food sources, and chemists scour the flora and fauna for compounds with seemingly magical properties. For instance, the piquia tree produces a compound that appears to be toxic to leaf-cutter ants, which cause millions of dollars of damage each year to South American agriculture. Such chemicals promise attractive alternatives to dangerous synthetic pesticides. Other jungle chemicals have already led to new treatments for hypertension and some forms of cancer. The lessons encoded in the genes of the Amazon's plants and animals may ultimately hold the key to solving a wide range of human problems.

Scientists are concerned that the destruction of the Amazon could lead to climatic chaos. Because of the huge volume of clouds it generates, the Amazon system plays a major role in the way the sun's heat is distributed around the globe. Any disturbance of this process could produce far-reaching, unpredictable effects. Moreover, the Amazon region stores at least 75 billion tons of carbon in its trees, which when burned spew carbon dioxide into the atmosphere. Since the air is already dangerously overburdened by carbon dioxide from the cars and factories of industrial nations, the torching of the Amazon could magnify the greenhouse effect—the trapping of heat by atmospheric CO_2. No one knows just what impact the buildup of CO_2 will have, but some scientists fear that the globe will begin to warm up, bringing on wrenching climatic changes.

The forest functions like a delicately balanced organism that recycles most of its nutrients and much of its moisture.[1] Wisps of steam float from the top of the endless palette of green as water evaporates off the upper leaves, cooling the trees as they collect the intense sunlight. Air currents over the forest gather this evaporation into clouds, which return the moisture to the system in torrential rains. Dead animals and vegetation decompose quickly, and the resulting nutrients move rapidly from the soil back to growing plants. The forest is such an efficient recycler that virtually no decaying matter seeps into the region's rivers.

In the early 1970s Brazil built the Trans-Amazon Highway, a system of roads that run west from the coastal city of Recife toward the Peruvian border. The idea was to prompt a land rush similar to the pioneering of the American West. To encourage settlers to brave the jungle, the government offered transportation and other incentives, allowing them to claim land that they had "improved" by cutting down the trees.

But for most of the roughly 8,000 families that heeded the government's call between 1970 and 1974, the dream turned into a bitter disappointment. The soil, unlike the rich sod in the Western United States, was so poor that crop yields began to deteriorate badly after three or four years. Most settlers eventually gave up and left. . . .

If the rain forest disappears, the process will begin at its edges. While the Amazon forest, as a whole, generates roughly half of its own moisture, the percentage is much higher in these western states, far from the Atlantic. This means that deforestation is likely to have a more dramatic impact on the climate

[1]Refer to the graphic on the next page for an illustration of this recycling process.

in the west than it would in the east. The process of deforestation could become self-perpetuating as heat, drying and wind cause the trees to die on their own. . . .

95 Perhaps the best hope for the forests' survival is the growing recognition that they are more valuable when left standing than when cut. Charles Peters of the Institute of Economic Botany at the New York Botanical Garden recently published the results of a three-year study that calculated the market value of rubber and exotic produce like the Aguaje palm fruit that can be harvested from the Amazonian jungle. The study, which appeared in the British journal *Nature*, 100 asserts that, over time, selling these products could yield more than twice the income of either cattle ranching or lumbering.

But if the burning of the forests goes on much longer, the damage may become irreversible. Long before the great rain forests are destroyed altogether, the impact of deforestation on climate could dramatically change the character of 105 the area, lead to mass extinctions of plant and animal species, and leave Brazil's poor to endure even greater misery than they do now. The people of the rest of the world, no less than the Brazilians, need the Amazon as a functioning system, and in the end, this is more important than the issue of who owns the forest. The Amazon may run through South America, but the responsibility for saving 110 the rain forests belongs to everyone.

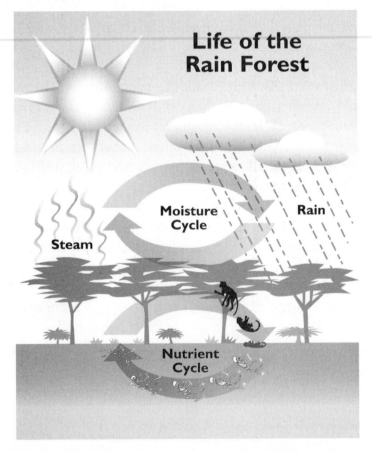

Reading Overview: Main Idea, Details, and Summary

Read the passage again. As you read, underline what you think are the most important ideas in the reading. Then, in one or two sentences, write the main idea of the reading. *Use your own words.*

Main Idea

_____

_____

_____

Details

Use the outline below to organize the information in the reading. Refer back to the information you underlined in the passage as a guide. When you have finished, write a brief summary of the reading. *Use your own words.*

PLAYING WITH FIRE

I. The Destruction of the Amazon Rain Forests

    A. by loggers, who cut down trees

    B.

    C.

    D.

    E.

II.

    A.

    B. It may change global weather patterns.

    C.

III. Overview of How Brazilian Rain Forests Became Endangered

    A.

    B.

    C. The poor soil failed in a few years.

IV. Advantages of Maintaining the Rain Forests

    A.

    B.

    C.

    D.

Summary

_____

_____

_____

_____

Statement Evaluation

Read the following statements. Then scan the article again quickly to find out if each sentence is **True (T), False (F),** or an **Inference (I).**

1. _____ According to this article, a large part of the Brazilian rain forest was burned last year.

2. _____ People have been destroying the Amazon rain forests for a long time.

3. _____ Industrialized nations can better afford to improve environmental conditions than can Third World nations.

4. _____ Few species of plants and animals live in the Amazon rain forest.

5. _____ The rain forests can be very important to mankind in ways that we are not yet aware of.

6. _____ Destruction of the Amazon can greatly affect the earth's weather patterns.

7. _____ The settlers of the Brazilian jungle in the early 1970s wanted to build a new life for themselves.

Read each question carefully. Either circle the letter or number of the correct answer or write your answer in the space provided.

1. Read lines 1–7.
   a. What is **"their annual rite of destruction"**?
      1. Raising crops and livestock
      2. Burning the Amazon rain forests
      3. The dark skies over western Brazil
   b. Why did the smoke grow so thick last year in Porto Velho?

      _____

2. In lines 9, 17, and elsewhere, there are ellipses (. . . .) at the end of the paragraph. These dots indicate that
   a. the last sentence is incomplete
   b. text has been deleted from the article
   c. there are exactly three sentences missing

3. Read lines 10–11. What does **inattention** mean?
   a. Not paying attention
   b. Paying attention

4. Read lines 19–23.
   a. **Time and again** means
      1. the last time
      2. many times
      3. at one time
   b. **Imminent** means
      1. something will happen a long time from now
      2. something will happen soon
   c. Why is the danger **"more real and imminent than ever before"**?

      _____

5. Read lines 32–35. **Moreover** means
   a. however
   b. although
   c. furthermore

6. Read lines 38–39. Why couldn't **all the biologists on earth fully describe its life forms**?
   a. Because there are so many life forms
   b. Because the life forms are hard to find
   c. Because the life forms are far away

7. Read lines 62–65.
   a. What is **the greenhouse effect**?

   _____

   b. In line 65, CO_2 is the chemical symbol for

   _____

8. Read lines 68–71. What does **recycle** mean?
   a. Go around in a circle again
   b. Extract and use again
   c. To fill up with moisture

9. Read lines 80–82. There are quotation marks (" ") around **improved** because the author
   a. wants to emphasize the improvement
   b. is stating a fact
   c. doesn't believe it really is improved

10. Read lines 90–92. **Deforestation** is
    a. the disappearance of the forest
    b. the climate of the forest
    c. the moisture of the forest

11. Read lines 99–101. What is *Nature*?

    _____

D. DICTIONARY SKILLS

Read the entry for each word and consider the context of the sentence from the passage. Write the definition that is appropriate for the context on the line next to the word. **Write the entry number, too, when appropriate.** Be prepared to explain your choice.

1. The "save the rain forest" movement has sparked a confrontation between rich industrial nations, which are **fresh** converts to the environmental cause, and the poorer nations of the Third World, which view outside interference as an assault on their sovereignty.

fresh: _____

> **fresh** \'fresh\ *adj* [ME, fr. OF *freis*, of Gmc origin; akin to OHG *frisc* fresh, OE *fersc* fresh] (13c) **1 a :** having its original qualities unimpaired: as (1): full of or renewed in vigor : REFRESHED ⟨rose ~ from a good night's sleep⟩ (2) : not stale, sour, or decayed ⟨~ bread⟩ (3) : not faded ⟨the lessons remain ~ in her memory⟩ (4) : not worn or rumpled ⟨a ~ white shirt⟩ **b :** not altered by processing ⟨~ vegetables⟩ **2 a :** not salt **b** (1) : free from taint : PURE ⟨ ~ air⟩ (2) *of wind* : moderately strong
> **3 a** (1) : experienced, made, or received newly or anew ⟨form ~ friendships⟩ (2) : ADDITIONAL, ANOTHER ⟨a ~ start⟩ **b :** ORIGINAL, VIVID ⟨a ~ portrayal⟩ **c :** lacking experience : RAW **d :** newly or just come or arrived ⟨~ from school⟩ **e :** having the milk flow recently established ⟨a ~ cow⟩ **4** [prob. by folk etymology fr. G. *frech*] : disposed to take liberties : IMPUDENT *syn* see NEW—**fresh·ly** *adv*—**fresh·ness** *n*

2. But now the danger is more real than ever before as loggers **level** trees and dams flood vast tracts of land.

level: _____

> **level** *vb* **-eled** *or* **-elled; -el·ing** *or* **-el·ling** \'le-və-liŋ, 'lev-liŋ\ *vt* (15c) **1 :** to make (a line or surface) horizontal : make flat or level ⟨~ a field⟩ ⟨~off a house lot⟩ **2 a :** to bring to a horizontal aiming position **b :** AIM, DIRECT ⟨~ed a charge of fraud⟩ **3 :** to bring to a common level or plane : EQUALIZE ⟨love ~s all ranks — W. S. Gilbert⟩ **4 a :** to lay level with or as if with the ground : RAZE **b :** to knock
> down ⟨~ed him with one punch⟩ **5 :** to make (as color) even or uniform **6 :** to find the heights of different points in (a piece of land) esp. with a surveyor's level ~ *vi* **1 :** to attain or come to a level ⟨the plane ~ed off at 10,000 feet⟩ **2 :** to aim a gun or other weapon horizontally **3 :** to bring persons or things to a level **4 :** to deal frankly and openly

\ə\abut \ᵊ\ kitten, \ər\ further \a\ ash \ā\ ace \ä\ mop, mar \aú \ out \ch\ chin \e\ bet \ē \ easy \g\go \i\ hit \ī \ ice \j\job \ŋ\sing \ō\ go \ò\ law \òi\ boy \th\ thin \t̲h̲\ the \ü\ loot \ú\ foot \y\ yet \zh\ vision \à, k̲, ⁿ, œ, œ̄, ᴜᴇ, ᵫ, ʸ\ *See Website below for* Pronunciation Guide.

3. Brazil built the Trans-Amazon Highway in the early 1970s. The idea was to **prompt** a land rush similar to the pioneering of the American West.

prompt: _____

> **¹prompt** \'präm(p)t\ *vt* [ME, fr. ML *promptare,* fr. L *promptus* prompt] (14c)
> **1 :** to move to action : INCITE **2 :** to assist (one acting or reciting) by suggesting or saying the next words of something forgotten or imperfectly learned : CUE **3 :** to serve as the inciting cause of — **prompt·er** *n*
> **²prompt** *adj* (1784) : of or relating to prompting actors
>
> **³prompt** *adj* [ME, fr. MF or L; MF, fr. L *promptus* ready, prompt, fr. pp. of *promere* to bring forth, fr. *pro-* forth + *emere* to take — more at REDEEM] (15c) **1 :** being ready and quick to act as occasion demands **2 :** performed readily or immediately ⟨~ assistance⟩ *syn* see QUICK — **prompt·ly** \'präm(p)t-lē, 'präm-plē\ *adv* —**prompt·ness** \'präm(p)t-nəs, 'prämp-nəs\ *n*
> **⁴prompt** *n, pl* prompts /'präm(p)ts, 'prämps\ (1597) 1 [¹*prompt*] : something that prompts : REMINDER 2 [³*prompt*] : a limit of time given for payment of an account for goods purchased; *also* : the contract by which this time is fixed

4. Charles Peters recently published the results of a three-year **study** that calculated the market value of rubber.

study: _____

> **study** \'stə-dē\ *n, pl* **stud·ies** [ME, *studie,* fr. OF *estudie,* fr. L *studium,* fr. *studēre* to devote oneself, study; prob. akin to L *tundere* to beat — more at CONTUSION] (14c)
> **1 :** **a** state of contemplation : REVERIE
> **2 a :** application of the mental faculties to the acquisition of knowledge ⟨years of ~⟩
> **b :** such application in a particular field or to a specific subject ⟨the ~ of Latin⟩ **c :** careful or extended consideration ⟨the proposal is under ~⟩
> **d** (1) : a careful examination or analysis of a phenomenon, development, or question (2) : the published report of such a study **3 :** a building or room devoted to study or literary pursuits **4 :** PURPOSE, INTENT
>
> **5 a :** a branch or department of learning : SUBJECT **b :** the activity or work of a student ⟨returning to her *studies* after vacation⟩ **c :** an object of study or deliberation ⟨every gesture a careful ~ — Marcia Davenport⟩ **d :** something attracting close attention or examination **6 :** a person who learns or memorizes something (as a part in a play) — usu. used with a qualifying adjective ⟨he's a fast ~⟩ **7 :** a literary or artistic production intended as a preliminary outline, an experimental interpretation, or an exploratory analysis of specific features or characteristics **8 :** a musical composition for the practice of a point of technique

By permission. From *Merriam-Webster's Online Dictionary* ©2002 by Merriam-Webster, Incorporated (www.Merriam-Webster.com).

E. Critical Thinking

Read each question carefully. Write your response in the space provided. Remember that there is no one correct answer. Your response depends on what **you** think.

1. The authors state that "the movement [to save the rain forest] has sparked a confrontation between rich industrial nations, which are fresh converts to the environmental cause, and the poorer nations of the Third World." Where are Third World countries located? Why do you think rich industrial nations are apparently more interested in environmental issues than are poorer Third World countries?

    _____

    _____

2. The authors are clearly in favor of preserving the Amazon rain forest. Are all their arguments persuasive? What are their strongest arguments? What are their weakest arguments?

    _____

    _____

    _____

    _____

3. The last sentence in the article states that "the responsibility for saving the rain forest belongs to everyone." What do you think the Brazilian government and the Brazilian people's attitude is about this statement? Explain your reasons.

    _____

    _____

    _____

4. According to the authors, the rain forest system extends into eight countries besides Brazil. Why do you think the authors focused on Brazil and didn't give equal mention to the other eight countries?

_____

_____

_____

Another Perspective

Taking Two Steps Back

by Mac Margolis
Newsweek

1   Imagine a great plume of smoke, big enough to stretch from the Rockies to Rhode Island, blotting out the sun and the moon. The Amazon, crown jewel of the world's rain forests, is burning—again. From June to November last year, tens of thousands of fires blazed over the two million square miles of the
5   Brazilian Amazon. Winds swept the pall of smoke across distant borders, shrouding the land and choking cities for hundreds of miles. Hospitals reported a surge in patients with bronchial problems. Smoke-blinded motorists smashed into each other on the highways. "It was like Los Angeles come to the Amazon," said Elaine Prins, a University of Wisconsin scientist studying the effect of the
10   burning on the world's climate.

    This was not the worst season of *queimadas* (burnings) ever. But the renewed binge was a cruel reminder to defenders of the Amazon that their battle was not yet won. The fires soured a recent memorial service for Francisco (Chico) Alves Mendes, the union leader and environmentalist whose protests
15   against land-clearing ranchers—and 1988 murder—turned the rape of rain

forests into a worldwide scandal. And the burning mocked the message of the 1992 Earth Summit in Rio de Janeiro, where Brazil answered critics by backing sweeping treaties to protect the environment. That year, all the attention seemed to be paying off. The government announced that the rate at which the rain forest was disappearing had been cut to half what it was in the 1980s, when an area the size of Massachusetts was lost every year.

The *queimadas* tradition, as old as agriculture, has proved almost impossible to uproot. And although the government took credit for curbing the practice, a sour economy may have had more to do with the progress in the early 1990s. "Ranchers simply did not have the money" to expand, argues Philip Fearnside of the Brazilian Institute of Amazon Studies. Now Brazil's economy is rebounding, and many farmers are beginning to expand again. And at the same time, drought made it easier to set fires and keep them going. Exactly how badly the fight against illegal land burning has gone this season is hard to say. Since 1992 the government has failed to come up with funds for an annual survey of the Amazon basin. "We were promised the funds, but they never came," says Volcker Kirchhoff, director of the Brazilian Space Institute. Still, institute researchers used satellite photos to document more than 150,000 fires throughout Brazil this season and no fewer than 95,000 in Amazonia.

Defenders of the Amazon have reawakened with a start. INFERNO ON THE GREEN FRONTIER, said a recent cover of *Veja*, the nation's leading news weekly. Ecology activists and defenders of Brazil's Indians have besieged President Fernando Henrique Cardoso with petitions. Surly crowds of Greens confronted the head of Brazil's environmental-protection agency, Raul Jungmann, on a recent trip to Washington.

The government calls it hype.[1] "The headlines are way out of proportion," Jungmann says. Besides making other arguments, government officials suggest that many of the latest fires were set to restore overgrown pastures and fields, not to clear virgin forest. Still, only now has Brasilia come up with $2.4 million for a detailed survey of the last three years' damage to the rain forest. It's already clear that protecting the Amazon basin may be as difficult as grabbing smoke.

---

[1]Hype is a term used, usually negatively, to describe exaggerated claims or publicity, often through the media.

1. What were some direct results of the most recent rain forest burnings?

_____

_____

_____

2. Who was Francisco Alves Mendes? Why do you think he might have been murdered?

_____

_____

3. a. What may be a reason that the number of burnings decreased in Brazil in the early 1990s?

_____

_____

   b. What may be one reason why the number of burnings has recently started to increase?

_____

_____

4. a. How does the government explain the latest fires?

_____

_____

   b. Do you think the author agrees or disagrees with the Brazilian government's explanation? Why?

_____

_____

1. Refer to the **Self-Evaluation of Reading Strategies** on page 282. Think about the strategies you used to help yourself understand "Playing with Fire." Check off the strategies you used. Think about the strategies you didn't use, and try to apply them to help yourself understand the readings that follow.

2. Look at the following chart carefully, then answer the questions that follow.

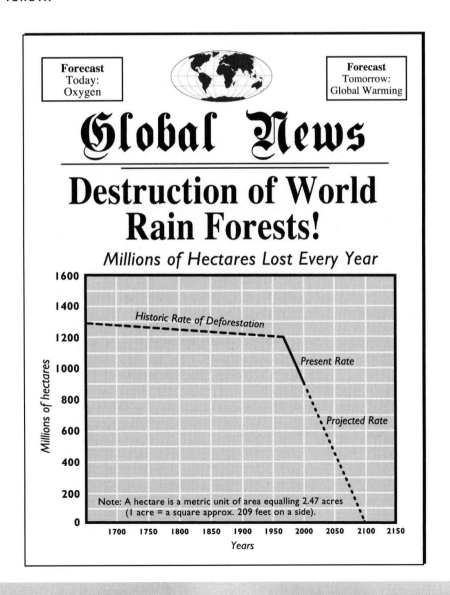

a. What does this chart illustrate?

_____

b. How many hectares of rain forest existed in the world in 1950?

_____

c. According to this chart, how many hectares of rain forest will exist in the world in the year 2100?

_____

d. The chart shows the projected rate of destruction of the rain forests between the years 2000 and 2100.

    1. What does **projected rate** mean?

    _____

    2. What is this rate based on?

    _____

    3. How can this rate be changed?

    _____

3. Form a panel of experts. Research the global effects of deforestation in the Amazon. Present and discuss solutions to the conflict between the development of Brazil and the preservation of the rain forest. Propose both short-term and long-range plans to satisfy both the immediate needs of Brazil and its citizens as well as the goals of environmentalists.

4. a. Prepare an interview with the president of Brazil. Be diplomatic. Ask questions about how the government is trying to improve conditions now and over the next few decades. Give the President the opportunity to respond to comments about Brazilian government policy and the deforestation of the Amazon jungle.

    b. Have one or two students volunteer to play the role of the president of Brazil. Have a panel of three or four students act as interviewers. With the other classmates as an audience, conduct an interview. When you are finished, review the interviewers' questions and the president's replies.

H. Topics for Discussion AND Writing

1. There are many different ways in which people are destroying our environment. There are also many different ways in which people are trying to preserve our environment. Give some examples of both actions.

2. What are some ways that this issue can be resolved with a compromise between environmentalists and people who are clearing the rain forests?

3. In the United States, many people are concerned about recycling waste. Do you think this is important? Why or why not? Is your country also concerned with recycling? Why or why not?

4. **Write in your journal.** Do you think it is important to save rain forests? Why or why not?

I. Cloze Quiz

Chapter 10: Playing with Fire

Read the passage below. Fill in the blanks with one word from the list. Use each word only once.

burning	deforestation	forests	products	roads
climatic	disappear	irreversible	rain	study
cutting	encourage	level	recycles	survival
danger	evaporation	moreover	river	world

The vast region of unbroken green that surrounds the Amazon

_____ and its tributaries has been under assault by settlers and
      (1)

developers for 400 years. Time and again, the forest has defied predictions

that it was doomed. But now the _____ is more real and
                                       (2)

imminent than ever before as loggers _____ trees, dams flood
                                           (3)

vast tracts of land, and gold miners poison rivers with mercury. In Peru the

_____ are being cleared to grow coca for cocaine production.
      (4)

"It's dangerous to say the forest will disappear by a particular year," says Philip

Fearnside of Brazil's National Institute for Research in the Amazon, "but unless

things change, the forest *will* _____."
                                    (5)

That would be more than a South American disaster. It would be an

incalculable catastrophe for the entire planet. If the forests vanish, so will

more than one million species. _____, the burning of the
                                        (6)

Amazon could have dramatic effects on global weather patterns—for

example, heightening the warming trend that may result from the

greenhouse effect....

Scientists are concerned that the destruction of the Amazon could lead to _____ chaos. Because of the huge volume of clouds it
(7)
generates, the Amazon system plays a major role in the way the sun's heat is distributed around the globe. Any disturbance of this process could produce far-reaching, unpredictable effects.

The forest functions like a delicately balanced organism that _____ most of its nutrients and much of its moisture. Wisps of
(8)
steam float from the top of the endless palette of green as water evaporates off the upper leaves, cooling the trees as they collect the intense sunlight. Air currents over the forest gather this _____ into clouds, which
(9)
return the moisture to the system in torrential rains. Dead animals and vegetation decompose quickly, and the resulting nutrients move rapidly from the soil back to growing plants. The forest is such an efficient recycler that virtually no decaying matter seeps into the region's rivers.

In the early 1970s Brazil built the Trans-Amazon Highway, a system of _____ that run west from the coastal city of Recife toward the
(10)
Peruvian border. To _____ settlers to brave the jungle, the
(11)
government offered transportation and other incentives, allowing them to claim land that they had "improved" by _____ down the trees.
(12)
If the _____ forest disappears, the process will begin at its
(13)
edges. While the Amazon forest, as a whole, generates roughly half of its own moisture, the percentage is much higher in these western states, far from the Atlantic. This means that _____ is likely to have a more dramatic
(14)
impact on the climate in the west than it would in the east. The process of deforestation could become self-perpetuating as heat, drying, and wind cause the trees to die on their own....

Perhaps the best hope for the forests' _____ is the growing
                                              (15)
recognition that they are more valuable when left standing than when cut.

Charles Peters of the Institute of Economic Botany recently published the

results of a three-year _____ that calculated the market value of
                              (16)
rubber and exotic produce like the Aguaje palm fruit that can be harvested

from the Amazonian jungle. The study, which appeared in the British journal

Nature, asserts that, over time, selling these _____ could yield
                                                       (17)
more than twice the income of either cattle ranching or lumbering.

But if the _____ of the forests goes on much longer, the
                 (18)
damage may become _____. Long before the great rain forests
                          (19)
are destroyed altogether, the impact of deforestation on climate could

dramatically change the character of the area, lead to mass extinctions of

plant and animal species, and leave Brazil's poor to endure even greater

misery than they do now. The people of the rest of the _____,
                                                              (20)
no less than the Brazilians, need the Amazon as a functioning system, and in

the end, this is more important than the issue of who owns the forest. The

Amazon may run through South America, but the responsibility for saving the

rain forests belongs to everyone.

Wilder Places for Wild Things

Prereading Preparation

1. Work with one or two partners. What do you know about traditional zoos? What do you know about modern zoos? Complete the following chart.

Traditional Zoos	Modern Zoos

2. Why do you think zoos have changed in these ways?

3. What do you like the most about traditional zoos? Modern zoos? What do you like the least? Why?

4. Read the title of this article. What aspect of zoos do you think the reading will focus on?

Wilder Places for Wild Things

by Sharon Begley with Karen Springen *in Chicago,* Jeanne Gordon *in Los Angeles,* Daniel Glick *in Washington,* and Howard Manley *in Atlanta*
Newsweek

1   The beavers at the Minnesota Zoo seem engaged in an unending task. Each week they fell scores of inch-thick young trees for their winter food supply. Each week zoo workers surreptitiously replace the downed trees, anchoring new ones in the iron holders so the animals can keep on cutting. Letting the beavers
5   do what comes naturally has paid off: Minnesota is one of the few zoos to get them to reproduce in captivity. The chimps at the St. Louis Zoo also work for a living: they poke stiff pieces of hay into an anthill to scoop out the baby food and honey that curators hide inside. Instead of idly awaiting banana handouts, the chimps get to manipulate tools, just as they do in the wild. Last year, when 13
10 gorillas moved into Zoo Atlanta's new $4.5 million rain forest, they mated and formed families—a rarity among captives. "Zoos have changed from being mere menageries to being celebrations of life," says John Gwynne of the Bronx Zoo. "As the wild places get smaller, the role of zoos gets larger, which means intensifying the naturalness of the experience for both visitors and animals."
15   Naturalistic zoos are hardly new: animals liberated from concrete cages have been romping on Bronx savannas since 1941. But as species become extinct at a rate unparalleled since the Cretaceous era and 100 acres of tropical forests vanish every minute, zoos are striving to make their settings match their new role as keepers of the biological flame. Since 1980 the nation's 143 accredited
20 zoos and aquariums have spent more than $1 billion on renovation and construction, much of it going to create habitats that immerse both animals and visitors in the sights, sounds, feel and smell of the wild. Today's best exhibits reproduce not just the look but also the function of a natural habitat: they encourage the residents to mate, to raise young and to develop the survival skills
25 they would need on the savannas of Africa or the slopes of the Andes. . . .
      Lately, curators have been making exhibits not only look real but sound real. At the Bronx Zoo's lush Jungle World the shrieks of gibbons, the

cacophony of crickets and the trills of hornbills emanate from 65 speakers. The zoo's resident audio expert, Tom Veltre, spent a month in Thailand stringing microphones and a mile of cables up and down mountains to capture the sounds of the jungle. Even though the animals figure out that the hoots and howls are coming from black boxes, and not from furry or feathered neighbors, the call of the wild can shape their behavior. At Healesville Sanctuary, outside Melbourne, Australia, nighttime sounds cue nocturnal platypuses when to sleep, says bio-acoustician Leslie Gilbert; realistic noises also snap gorillas out of stress-induced lethargy.

"Natural" is now going beyond sight and sound to include everything from weather to activity patterns. Every day 11 rainstorms hit Tropic World at the Brookfield Zoo outside Chicago, prompting the monkeys to drop from their vines and scamper for cover amid cliffs, 50-foot-high gunite trees and 6,000 tropical plants. Regardless of the climate, the monkeys exhibit an array of behaviors never displayed in cages, such as rustling bushes to define their territories. At the San Diego Zoo's Sun Bear Forest, lion-tailed macaques are surrounded by jungle vines and cascading waterfalls. As soon as these highly endangered monkeys moved in last month, they fanned out and began foraging for fruit and other dainties left by the curators. They even respond to the dominant male's alarm call by clustering around him—something keepers had never seen. At Seattle's Woodland Park Zoo, elephants in the exhibit that opened last month roll and stack logs just as they do in a Thai logging camp. The task relieves the pachyderms' boredom.

Curators of rare species are focusing on how to induce one particular natural behavior—reproduction. At New York's Central Park Zoo, which reopened last year after a multimillion-dollar overhaul, the lights in the penguin house mimic seasonal changes in the austral day and night, which serve as a crucial cue for the birds' breeding cycle. At the San Diego Wild Animal Park, people are confined to cages (an electric monorail), and 2,600 animals roam free on 700 acres of veld and savanna. A white rhino that had never mated during 10 years at the San Diego Zoo has sired 55 offspring since moving into a 110-acre area at the park 17 years ago. "The difference is that he has room to mark out his territory and a harem [of 20] from which to choose," says spokesman Tom Hanscom. Getting flamingos to breed was simply a matter of providing more neighbors. For reasons curators can't explain, the leggy pink birds never bred when they lived in two flocks of 50. But when merged into a group of 100 they began to build little mud mounds in the lake shallows on which to lay their eggs.

Once fiercely competitive, most American zoos now participate in species-survival programs, intricate dating games for animals living far apart. Coordinated by the American Association of Zoological Parks and Aquariums, the SSP's rely on studbooks that keep track of zoo animals' age and ancestry, helping curators determine how to pair up males and females from member zoos to maintain the species' health and avoid inbreeding. Animals move back and forth between zoos to ensure the best genetic mix. Right now Indian rhinos from the Oklahoma City and National zoos are cozying up to the Bronx Zoo's female.

Without such programs, many species would be extinct. "Zoos are becoming the last hope for a number of endangered species," says Ronald Tilson of the Minnesota Zoo. Indeed, there are more Siberian tigers in America's zoos than on Russia's northern tundra. For all their breeding successes, though, zoos will become little more than Noah's arks if nature continues to give way to pavement. That's why the new naturalistic settings are designed with people in mind, too. "Part of a zoo's reason for being is to inform the public of the marvelous things that occur on this planet," says Warren Thomas, director of the Los Angeles Zoo. "You do that by re-creating the environment that shaped these animals." In zoo parlance, it's called habitat immersion: getting visitors curious and excited about wild places and teaching them that habitat loss is the single greatest threat to wild animals today.

In the rare cases when animals bred in captivity do have an ancestral home to return to, zoos are trying to oblige them. "The closer you come to mimicking nature in captivity, the easier that is," says primate curator Ann Baker of Brookfield. Already the Bronx Zoo has returned condors to the Andes. Scientists at the National Zoo in Washington taught a group of golden lion tamarins survival skills, such as how to forage and to heed warning calls, and have released 67 into a reserve near Rio de Janeiro since 1984. Although 35 died, others not only survived but mated; so far, the freed animals have produced 13 surviving offspring. The San Diego Park has returned 49 oryxes—rare antelopes—to Oman, Jordan and Israel, where the graceful creatures have bred successfully. Black-foot ferrets, which a few years ago had dwindled to only 17 in the wild, have proliferated to 125 in captivity, and scientists plan to release the animals into prairie-dog territories in the Great Plains in a few years.

With every animal that moves onto the endangered species list, or drops off it by extinction, zoos assume greater importance. About 120 million people will visit U.S. zoos this year, giving curators 120 million chances to spread the conservation gospel. By showing how animals are shaped and supported by their environment, "zoos are trying to protect wild places as well as wild things," says Zoo Atlanta director Terry Maple. For as the wild places go, so go the wild animals.

Read the passage again. As you read, underline what you think are the most important ideas in the reading. Then, in one or two sentences, write the main idea of the reading. *Use your own words.*

Main Idea

_____

_____

_____

Details

Use the outline below to organize the information in the reading. Refer back to the information you underlined in the passage as a guide. When you have finished, write a brief summary of the reading. *Use your own words.*

WILDER PLACES FOR WILD THINGS

I. Examples of Animal Behavior in Naturalistic Settings

    A.

    B.

    C.

II. Zoos Re-create Animals' Natural Environment

    What zoos do:

    Examples:

    Results:

III.

    A. Purpose of the SSPs

        1.

        2.

        3.

    B.

        1.

        2.   The release of golden lion tamarins into a reserve in Brazil.

        3.

Summary

_____

_____

_____

_____

B. Statement Evaluation

Read the following statements. Then scan the article again quickly to find out if each sentence is **True (T), False (F),** or an **Opinion (O).**

1. _____ Beavers reproduce in most zoos.

2. _____ At the Minnesota Zoo, animals are able to get their own food instead of being fed.

3. _____ Naturalistic zoos are better than traditional zoos.

4. _____ Modern zoos do not encourage animals to learn how to survive in the wild.

5. _____ Zoo curators are arranging for animals from different zoos to reproduce together.

6. _____ Naturalistic zoos give people important information about an animal's natural environment.

7. _____ Animals are happier in naturalistic zoos than they are in traditional zoos.

Read each question carefully. Either circle the letter or number of the correct answer or write your answer in the space provided.

1. Read lines 6–8.
   a. What do the chimps at this zoo **work for**?

      _____

   b. What follows the colon (:)?
      1. An explanation
      2. An example
      3. A new idea

2. Read lines 9–11. What is **a rarity among captives**?

   _____

3. Read lines 13–14. **"The role of zoos gets larger"** means
   a. zoos are getting bigger
   b. zoos are becoming more important
   c. wild places are getting smaller

4. Read lines 26–28. Where do the realistic sounds in the zoos come from?
   a. The jungle
   b. The animals
   c. The speakers

5. Read lines 37–46.
   a. Why is the word **natural** in quotation marks (" ")?

      _____

   b. What does **regardless of** mean?
      1. in spite of
      2. instead of
      3. in addition to

    c. What does **these highly endangered monkeys** refer to?

    _____

6. Read lines 48–50.

    a. What word is a synonym for **pachyderms**?

    _____

    b. What does **just as** mean?

        1. only
        2. in the same way
        3. because of

7. Read lines 65–71. What is an **SSP**?

    _____

8. Read lines 86–87. **"Zoos are trying to oblige them"** means that zoos

    a. want to return animals to their natural environment

    b. want to keep the animals in captivity

    c. are trying to get the animals to reproduce

9. Read lines 96–98. What are **dwindled** and **proliferated**?

    a. Numbers

    b. Synonyms

    c. Antonyms

10. Read lines 99–100.

    a. Animals that **drop off it by extinction**

        1. all die
        2. survive
        3. increase

    b. Read lines 104 and 105. This sentence means that when the animals' natural environment disappears,

        1. the animals will reproduce
        2. the animals will disappear, too
        3. the animals will prefer to live in zoos

D. DICTIONARY SKILLS

Read the entry for each word and consider the context of the sentence from the passage. Write the definition that is appropriate for the context on the line next to the word. **Write the entry number, too, when appropriate.** Be prepared to explain your choice.

1. Seasonal changes in the austral day and night serve as a crucial **cue** for the penguins' breeding cycle.

    cue: _____

    > **¹cue** \'kyü\ *n* [ME *cu* half a farthing (spelled form of *q,* abbr. for L *quadrans* quarter of an as)] (ca. 1755) : the letter *q*
    > **²cue** *n* [prob. fr. *qu,* abbr (used as a direction in actors' copies of plays) of L *quando* when] (1553) **1 a :** a signal (as a word, phrase, or bit of stage business) to a performer to begin a specific speech or action **b :** something serving a comparable purpose : HINT **2 :** a feature indicating the nature of something perceived **3** *archaic :* the part one has to perform in or as if in a play **4** *archaic :* MOOD, HUMOR
    >
    > **³cue** *vt* **cued; cu·ing** *or* **cue·ing** (1922) **1 :** to give a cue to : PROMPT **2 :** to insert into a continuous performance ⟨~ in sound effects⟩
    > **⁴cue** *n* [F *queue,* lit. tail, fr. L *cauda*] (ca. 1749) **1 a :** a leather-tipped tapering rod for striking the cue ball (as in billiards and pool) **b :** a long-handled instrument with a concave head for shoving disks in shuffleboard **2 :** QUEUE 2
    > **⁵cue** *vb* **cued; cu·ing** *or* **cue·ing** *vt* (ca. 1784) **1 :** QUEUE **2 :** to strike with a cue ~ *vi* **1 :** QUEUE **2 :** to use a cue

2. Since 1980 the nation's 143 accredited zoos and aquariums have spent more than $1 billion on renovation and construction, much of it going to create habitats that **immerse** both animals and visitors in the sights, sounds, feel and smell of the wild.

    Part of a zoo's reason for being is to inform the public. You do that by re-creating the environment that shaped these animals. This is called habitat **immersion:** getting visitors curious and excited about wild places.

    immerse: _____

    > **im·merse** \i-'mərs\ *vt* **im·mersed; im·mers·ing** [ME, fr. L *immersus,* pp. of *immergere,* fr. *in-* + *mergere* to merge] (15c) **1 :** to plunge into something that surrounds or covers; *esp :* to plunge or dip into a fluid **2 :** ENGROSS, ABSORB ⟨completely *immersed* in his work⟩ **3 :** to baptize by immersion

3. The lights in the penguin house **mimic** seasonal changes in the austral day and night.

   The closer you can **mimic** nature in captivity, the easier it is to return animals to the wild.

   mimic: _____

   > ¹**mim·ic** \'mi-mik\ *n* (1590) **1 :** MIME
   > **2 :** one that mimics
   > ²**mimic** *adj* [L *mimicus*, fr. Gk *mimikos*, fr. *mimos* mime] (1598) **1 a :** IMITATIVE
   > **b :** IMITATION, MOCK ⟨a ~ battle⟩ **2 :** of or relating to mime or mimicry
   > ³**mimic** *vt* **mim·icked** \-mikt\;
   > **mim·ick·ing** (1687) **1 :** to imitate closely : APE **2 :** to ridicule by imitation
   > **3 :** SIMULATE **4 :** to resemble by biological mimicry *syn* see COPY

4. When animals bred in captivity have a home to return to, zoos are trying to **oblige** them. Already the Bronx Zoo has returned condors to the Andes.

   oblige: _____

   > **oblige** \ə-'blīj\ *vb* **obliged; oblig·ing**
   > [ME, fr. OF *obliger,* fr. L *obligare,* lit., to bind to, fr. *ob-* toward + *ligare* to bind—more at LIGATURE] *vt* (14c) **1 :** to constrain by physical, moral, or legal force or by the exigencies of circumstance ⟨*obliged* to find a job⟩ **2 a :** to put in one's debt by a favor or service ⟨we are much *obliged* for your help⟩
   > **b :** to do a favor for ⟨always read to ~ a friend⟩ ~ *vi* : to do something as or as if a favor *syn* see FORCE— **oblig·er** *n*

E. Critical Thinking

Read each question carefully. Write your response in the space provided. Remember that there is no one correct answer. Your response depends on what **you** think.

1. Why do you think zoos have taken on the responsibility of preserving endangered species?

   _____

   _____

   _____

2. The authors state that most American zoos were **"once fiercely competitive."** Why do you think zoos were competitive? Why do you think they are not competitive anymore?

   _____

   _____

   _____

3. Why are there more Siberian tigers in America's zoos than there are in Russia's northern tundra?

   _____

   _____

   _____

4. Why do zoos assume greater importance as more animals move onto the endangered species list?

   _____

   _____

Another Perspective

Predators on the Prowl

by Marc Peyser with Daniel Glick
Newsweek

1   For Iris Kenna, Cuyamaga Rancho State Park near San Diego was like a second home. By day, she strolled its fields in search of exotic birds. At night, the 56-year-old high-school counselor sometimes slept under the stars. But one morning exactly a year ago, Kenna encountered something unfamiliar, and it saw
5   her first. Without warning, a 140-pound male mountain lion pounced on her from behind. The struggle was brief. The animal dragged the dying 5-foot-4 Kenna into dense brush to hide her from competing predators. Rangers found her only after two hikers spotted a pair of glasses, a backpack and a human tooth by the path she had been on. The rangers followed a trail of her clothes for 30
10   yards until they came to Kenna's body. The back of her scalp was ripped off; the rest of her was riddled with bites. No one had heard a scream, or even a roar.
     Kenna is the most vivid symbol of an angry, shifting debate over how people and predators can coexist. In the high-growth Western states, many residents love living near the wild, and they are inclined to preserve it no matter what the
15   risks. But violent deaths like Kenna's—and a string of other mountain-lion attacks—are making a powerful case for fighting back. Californians will vote in

March on opening the way to mountain-lion hunting, which has been prohibited there for more than 20 years.[1] But Oregon, Arizona and Colorado recently changed their hunting laws to ensure that predatory animals—including bears, wolves and coyotes—would be protected. "It's overwhelmingly popular to have these animals in our ecosystems," says Tom Dougherty of the National Wildlife Federation. "But if they're in your backyard, some people aren't loving it."

The most acute mountain-lion problem is in California. That's partly because the state's human population has doubled every 25 years this century. As more people built more houses, they usurped territory once largely inhabited by wild animals. But the mountain lion (alternately called cougar, puma and panther) has also been questionably served by environmentalists. In 1972, preservation-minded Californians banned hunting the majestic animals (except when they pose an imminent danger to people or livestock). The cougar population ballooned, from an estimated 2,400 lions to 6,000 today. Without hunters to thin the ranks, increased competition for food has sent hungry mountain lions to suburban backyards, shopping centers and elementary schools in search of nourishment—a deer or, lacking that, a dog. Even children have been mauled. "People are afraid to go on a picnic without taking a firearm," says state Senator Timi Leslie, a prominent anti-cougar advocate. In the wake of Kenna's death, Gov. Pete Wilson authorized the March ballot initiative—one that could lead to controlling the cougar population.

But in other places, sentiment favors animals at least as much as people. A survey of Coloradans living near the Rockies found that 80 percent believe that development in mountain-lion territory should be restricted. What's more, when wildlife authorities killed the cougar that killed a woman named Barbara Schoener in California in 1994, donors raised $21,000 to care for the cougar's cub—but only $9,000 for Schoener's two children.

[1]Postscript: In March, Californians once again voted against legalization of mountain-lion hunting.

F.

Questions for "Predators on the Prowl"

1. How did Iris Kenna die?

   _____

   _____

2. a. What proposed law must Californians decide upon?

   _____

   _____

   b. What is the purpose of this proposed law?

   _____

   _____

   c. Why are some people against this proposed law?

   _____

   _____

3. Why has the mountain-lion problem in California increased over the years?

   _____

   _____

   _____

4. How do most people in Colorado feel about the mountain lions? What example do the authors give to support their belief?

_____

_____

5. What do you think is the authors' opinion of the mountain-lion situation in the western United States? Why do you think so?

_____

_____

_____

G.   Follow-up Activities

1. Refer to the **Self-Evaluation of Reading Strategies** on page 282. Think about the strategies you used to help yourself understand "Wilder Places for Wild Things." Check off the strategies you used. Think about the strategies you didn't use, and try to apply them to help yourself understand the readings that follow.

2. Work in small groups. You are journalists for a local television station in San Diego. You have been assigned to cover the use of state and municipal (i.e., local) funds that have recently been allocated to the San Diego Zoo. Prepare an interview with the curator of the San Diego Zoo. In your interview, include questions about the justification of this amount of money for the zoo's long-range goals. For example, what will the zoo do with the money? Why should the zoo have gotten such funding? Why should the residents of San Diego and California support such a project? Remember to add some questions of your own. When you have finished, exchange your questions with another group of classmates' questions. Try to answer their questions as they try to answer yours. When you are finished, compare your responses. Have the "curators" answered the "interviewers" questions convincingly?

3. Work in small groups. What do you think of the problem described in "Predators on the Prowl"? How do you think the problem can be solved? Write a list of your group's suggestions. Then compare your list with your classmates'. Decide which two or three suggestions are the best solutions.

H. *Topics for Discussion* AND *Writing*

1. According to the article, many endangered species raised in zoos were released into the wild. Many of these animals died. Do you think it is good practice for zoos to release these endangered animals and risk their death in the wild? Discuss your opinion with your classmates.

2. Compare the zoos in this country with zoos in your country and in other countries. How are they similar? How are they different?

3. Many zoo curators and other specialists are trying to save species of animals from extinction. Do you think it is important to try to preserve these animals? Explain your point of view.

4. **Write in your journal.** Refer to "Predators on the Prowl." Think about the amount of money that was raised for the victim's two children compared to the money raised for the cougar's cub. What is your opinion about this?

Cloze Quiz

Chapter 11: Wilder Places for Wild Things

Read the passage below. Fill in the blanks with one word from the list. Use each word only once.

beavers	elephants	mated	reproduce	vanish
behaviors	extinct	mimic	role	visitors
construction	habitats	natural	smaller	weather
cues	hide	replace	sounds	work

The beavers at the Minnesota Zoo seem engaged in an unending task. Each week they fell scores of inch-thick young trees for their winter food supply. Each week zoo workers _____ the downed trees, (1) anchoring new ones in the iron holders so the animals can keep on cutting. Letting the _____ do what comes naturally has paid off: (2) Minnesota is one of the few zoos to get them to _____ in (3) captivity. The chimps at the St. Louis Zoo also _____ for a living: (4) they poke stiff pieces of hay into an anthill to scoop out the baby food and honey that curators _____ inside. Instead of idly awaiting (5) banana handouts, the chimps get to manipulate tools, just as they do in the wild. Last year, when 13 gorillas moved into Zoo Atlanta's new $4.5 million rain forest, they _____ and formed families—a rarity among (6) captives. "Zoos have changed from being mere menageries to being celebrations of life," says John Gwynne of the Bronx Zoo. "As the wild places get _____, the role of zoos gets larger, which means intensifying (7) the naturalness of the experience for both _____ and animals." (8)

Naturalistic zoos are hardly new; animals liberated from concrete cages have been romping on Bronx savannas since 1941. But as species become _____ at a rate unparalleled since the Cretaceous era and 100
(9)
acres of tropical forests _____ every minute, zoos are striving to
(10)
make their settings match their new _____ as keepers of the
(11)
biological flame. Since 1980 the nation's 143 accredited zoos and aquariums have spent more than $1 billion on renovation and _____, much
(12)
of it going to create _____ that immerse both animals and
(13)
visitors in the sights, _____, feel and smell of the wild. Today's
(14)
best exhibits reproduce not just the look but also the function of a _____ habitat: they encourage the residents to mate, to raise
(15)
young and to develop the survival skills they would need on the savannas of Africa or the slopes of the Andes. . . .

"Natural" is now going beyond sight and sound to include everything from _____ to activity patterns. Every day 11 rainstorms hit
(16)
Tropic World at the Brookfield Zoo outside Chicago, prompting the monkeys to drop from their vines and scamper for cover amid cliffs, 50-foot-high trees and 6,000 tropical plants. Regardless of the climate, the monkeys exhibit an array of _____ never displayed in cages, such as rustling bushes
(17)
to define their territories. At Seattle's Woodland Park Zoo, _____
(18)
in the exhibit that opened last month roll and stack logs just as they do in a Thai logging camp. The task relieves the pachyderms' boredom.

Curators of rare species are focusing on how to induce one particular natural behavior—reproduction. At New York's Central Park Zoo, which reopened last year after a multimillion-dollar overhaul, the lights in the penguin house _____ seasonal changes in the austral day and
(19)

night, which serve as a crucial _____ for the birds' breeding
(20)
cycle. At the San Diego Wild Animal Park, people are confined to cages (an
electric monorail), and 2,600 animals roam free on 700 acres of veld and
savanna. A white rhino that had never mated during 10 years at the San
Diego Zoo has sired 55 offspring since moving into a 110-acre area at the
park 17 years ago.

12

A Nuclear Graveyard

Prereading Preparation

One of the greatest environmental concerns facing the world today is the disposal of nuclear waste. Much of this waste comes from nuclear power plants. (Refer to the illustration on page 283. You may want to do the exercise related to the illustration before you read the article.) In the United States, for example, the government is looking for a safe place to bury its nuclear waste. Currently the federal government is focusing on one particular site: the Yucca Mountains in the state of Nevada. Read the following paragraph, which is the first part of the article. Then answer the questions.

Introduction: A Nuclear Graveyard

1
   The apocalyptic scenario begins with an earthquake near Yucca Mountain, a barren ridge 90 miles northwest of Las Vegas that is the burial site for the nation's most lethal nuclear waste. The tremor is minor; but fresh movement in the earth's crust causes ground water to well up suddenly, flooding the
5
repository. Soon, a lethal brew of nuclear poisons seeps into the water that flows underground to nearby Death Valley. Insects, birds and animals drink at the valley's contaminated springs, and slowly the radioactivity spreads into the biosphere. "It would be a terrible disaster," says Charles Archambeau, a geophysicist at the University of Colorado.

1. What does this paragraph describe?
   a. It describes what may happen if there is an earthquake at the place where the nuclear waste is buried.
   b. It describes what happens during all earthquakes.

2. Work with a partner to complete the following flowchart. According to the above paragraph, what is the chain of events that would lead to **"radioactivity spreading into the biosphere"**?

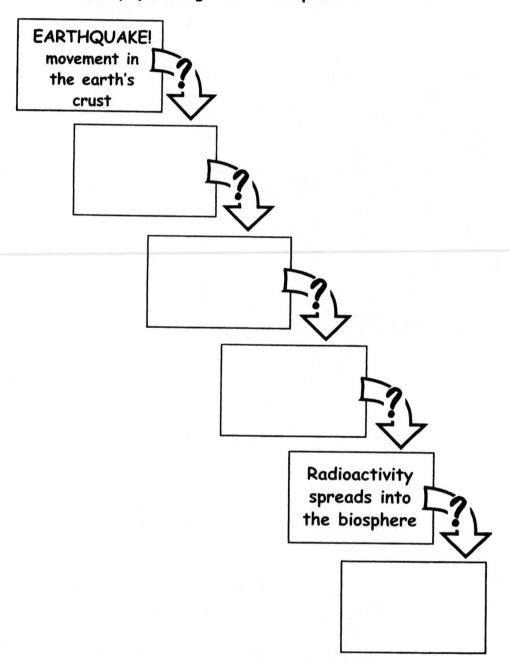

3. Do you think there is a better way for a country to dispose of its nuclear waste? Write your ideas on the lines below. Then discuss them with your classmates. Make a list of the class's solutions. Then continue reading the article.

_____

_____

_____

_____

A Nuclear Graveyard (continued)

by Betsy Carpenter
U.S. News & World Report

10   Much has been made of this scary scenario by the state of Nevada, which is fighting the federal government's plan to bury all the nation's high-level nuclear refuse inside Yucca Mountain. But in fact, the risk to Nevadans may be overstated. Increasingly, experts view this arid, desolate ridge as a good spot for a permanent nuclear graveyard. The threat to Americans posed by the federal

15   government's bungled attempts to find a safe burial site for the waste looms large, however. Thousands of tons of highly radioactive spent fuel rods rest temporarily today in pools of water—some dangerously overcrowded—near nuclear power plants around the country. At the nation's weapons factories, corroding tanks are leaking nuclear poisons into the ground water. This

20   stalemate over nuclear waste is strangling the nuclear power industry, and experts are increasingly troubled by the possibility that nuclear waste could become the weapon of choice for a new breed of terrorist.

The twin virtues of the Yucca Mountain site are its remoteness and aridity. From the summit, the only sign of civilization is the dusty trace of a dirt road

25   cutting across a brown, barren valley. The ridge is located on the southwest corner of the Nevada Test Site, where the government explodes nuclear weapons, so access is tightly restricted. Sagebrush, creosote bushes and other desert plants attest to the locale's remarkable dryness.

Indeed, only six inches of rain fall on the mountain each year, and most of

30   the moisture evaporates, leaving as little as one fiftieth of an inch to soak into the ground. The water table is unusually deep, more than one third of a mile below the surface. According to the Department of Energy, which is charged with building the repository, nuclear waste could be buried far beneath the ground yet still rest safely above the ground water.

Geological Turmoil

The landscape also provides stark reminders of why critics are so concerned. To the southeast stands Busted Butte, a peak that was sheared in half long ago by earthquakes; to the west, four smooth-sloped volcanoes rise out of a high valley. The reason for the geological turmoil is that immense forces inside the earth are stretching the earth's crust apart here, much like a sheet of rubber. Earthquakes relieve the strain, but they also disrupt the water table: As the crust snaps back into shape, rocks contract, and water that has seeped deep into fractures is forced up toward the surface.

The repository site must be capable of isolating atomic waste for 10,000 years. By all accounts, there could be a frightful mess if the poisons escaped the site. In a few years, the nation will have produced 48,000 tons of high-level nuclear waste, the most concentrated products of the nuclear era. Every speck of this refuse is intensely poisonous.

Water is the worst enemy of buried nuclear waste. If water did find its way into the repository, it would corrode the storage canisters and hasten the escape of radioactive particles through the rock. Scientists cannot know absolutely whether ground water will well up under Yucca Mountain during the next 10,000 years. The calculation simply has too many unknowns: A new ice age, global climate change, erosion, volcanoes and earthquakes all could affect the water table. To gauge the probabilities, scientists reconstruct the past. If the water table has risen in the past, scientists assume, it is likely to do so again.

Jerry Szymanski, a maverick engineering geologist with the Department of Energy (DOE), claims that he has rock-hard evidence that ground water was once as much as 500 meters higher than it is today. He has devoted the past seven years to blowing the whistle on what he believes to be a fatally flawed site, and his arguments have received extensive media attention. Szymanski bases his case largely on the presence of thick, cream-colored veins of a crystalline deposit, known as calcite, that plunge through the mottled, grey bedrock of Yucca Mountain. In Szymanski's view, these calcite brands must have been deposited slowly, layer by layer, as mineral-rich ground water welled up into fractures in the rock. "Ground water will rise again in the next 10,000 years," he says flatly. "It is as certain as death."

Other Voices

But according to an increasing number of earth scientists, it is not the site but Szymanski's conclusion that is fatally flawed. Largely as a result of Szymanski's warnings, the National Academy of Sciences convened a panel of researchers to evaluate the risks associated with ground water. The panel has not yet released its final report, but already many members are convinced that there is no evidence for Szymanski's hypothesis—but there are several good reasons to doubt it. Most believe that rainwater, not upwelling ground water, probably produced the calcite veins. One strong reason to suspect precipitation, says Bob Fournier, a geologist with the United States Geological Survey in Menlo Park, California, is that the calcite veins around Yucca Mountain do not exhibit the common structural characteristics of ancient springs. For instance, upwelling water typically leaves snowy-white mounds of calcite on the ground, deposits that are formed when the water evaporates; few such signatures can be found at Yucca Mountain.

Preliminary chemical analyses also suggest that the disputed calcites were deposited by rainwater. Doug Rumble, a geochemist at the Carnegie Institution in Washington, D.C., analyzed several existing studies of the chemical character of the disputed Yucca Mountain veins, the ground water underneath and ancient and modern ground water deposits; he found no evidence that the calcites at Yucca are or ever were caused by ground water.

Somewhat surprisingly, scientists are much more concerned about ground water seepage than they are about more dramatic geologic events like volcanoes and earthquakes. Fresh eruptions from the small volcanoes along Yucca Mountain's western flank probably wouldn't threaten the repository because the flows would be small and localized, most geologists believe. The possibility of a direct hit, a new upwelling of magma right beneath the repository, is minute, they say.

Earthquakes are not a major concern either, scientists contend. Though Yucca Mountain is ringed with seismic faults, many of them known to be active, most geologists do not worry that shock waves from an earthquake could rupture the repository. Experience with tremors throughout the world has shown unequivocally that tunnels and mines stand up well to them. For instance, a devastating earthquake killed 250,000 people in a coal-mining city in China in 1976. Reportedly, workers in the mines below did not feel even the slightest tremor. Closer to home, underground nuclear explosions on the nearby test site have shown that tunnels can withstand forces even greater than those produced by earthquakes.

"From what we know now, I would feel quite comfortable with Yucca Mountain," says George Thompson, a geologist at Stanford University and a member of the National Academy of Sciences' panel. Though panel members agree that a lot more study is needed, most do not believe that the geological complexity disqualifies the site. Explains Clarence Allen, a geologist from Caltech in Pasadena, California, "If you asked me to find a site with fewer earthquakes or volcanoes, I could. But an overall better site? I'm not so sure."

Maintaining the pretense of an unassailable site also has had an unfortunate impact on the design of the repository. Currently, the DOE plans to build a complex that would be backfilled and sealed off after it had been loaded to capacity. Experts like Stanford's George Thompson assert that this approach is foolish. Instead, the government should design the facility so that the waste could be easily retrieved if the repository failed.

Congress must have had an inkling that forcing the project on Nevada might not work out in the end. In the same bill that designated Yucca Mountain the sole candidate for site evaluation, Congress established the Office of the U.S. Nuclear Waste Negotiator, which is charged with finding a willing state or Indian tribe[1] to host the repository. David Leroy, who took the job last summer, is putting together a package of incentives and assurances that he hopes will lure several state or tribal leaders to the bargaining table. The assurances include promises of local participation in deciding how the facility is operated and the freedom to back out of the evaluation process at any time. When it comes to incentives the sky's the limit. Highways? Airports? Schools? Harbor cleanups? "You tell me what the problem is, and let's see if we can address it," he says. Who knows, maybe Leroy can find a way to make even cynical Nevadans willing to host the repository.

[1]In the United States, Indian (Native American) tribes own their land, called *reservations*. The tribe holds decision-making power as to what takes place on tribal land. They are not under the jurisdiction of the federal government or of the government of the state in which the reservation is located.

Read the passage again. As you read, underline what you think are the most important ideas in the reading. Then, in one or two sentences, write the main idea of the reading. *Use your own words.*

Main Idea

_____

_____

_____

Details

Use the chart below to organize the information in the article. Refer back to the information you underlined in the passage as a guide. When you have finished, write a brief summary of the reading. *Use your own words.*

A NUCLEAR GRAVEYARD

The Nuclear Repository Controversy: To Use or Not to Use the Yucca Mountain Site	
Arguments Against Using This Site	Arguments in Favor of Using This Site

Summary

_____

_____

_____

_____

B. Statement Evaluation

Read the following statements. Then scan the article again quickly to find out if each sentence is **True (T), False (F),** or an **Inference (I).**

1. _____ Experts believe that Yucca Mountain is a good place to bury nuclear waste.

2. _____ There is a great deal of rain on the mountain every year.

3. _____ The greatest danger to nuclear waste is water.

4. _____ The presence of calcite has led to many arguments about the safety of Yucca Mountain as a nuclear waste repository site.

5. _____ Earthquake tremors are always felt far below the surface of the earth.

6. _____ Most members of the National Academy of Sciences' panel believe that the Yucca Mountain site may be a good place for nuclear waste disposal.

7. _____ Some Indian tribes live near Yucca Mountain.

Read each question carefully. Either circle the letter or number of the correct answer or write your answer in the space provided.

1. In line 10, what does **this scary scenario** refer to?

   _____

   _____

2. Read lines 12–13.

   a. **"The risk to Nevadans may be overstated." To overstate** means
      1. to make something seem greater than it really is
      2. to make something seem smaller than it really is

   b. Who are **Nevadans**?

      _____

3. Read lines 23–28.

   a. **Remoteness** means
      1. close to people
      2. far away from people

   b. How do you know?

      _____

   c. In this paragraph, what is a synonym of **aridity**?

      _____

4. Read lines 32–34. What is a **repository**?
   a. Nuclear waste
   b. A safe place for the nuclear waste
   c. The ground water above the nuclear waste

5. Read lines 43–47. Which words are synonyms of **waste**?

   _____

6. Read lines 48–55.

    a. Why do scientists reconstruct the past?

        1. To try to predict what may happen in the future

        2. To help them understand the past

    b. **"It is likely to do so again"** means

        1. there may be more earthquakes

        2. the water table may rise again

        3. the climate may change again

7. Read lines 58–60. **Blowing the whistle** means

    a. making music

    b. giving false information

    c. revealing the truth

8. Read lines 73–77. What is one type of **precipitation** referred to in these lines?

_____

9. Read lines 87–93.

    a. In this paragraph, what is another way of saying **lava flow from a volcano**?

_____

    b. **"The possibility of a direct hit . . . is minute"** means

        1. there is a very small chance

        2. there is a very big chance

10. Read lines 94–103.

    a. **Unequivocally** means

        1. probably

        2. definitely

        3. slightly

    b. What is an example of the **unequivocal** evidence that tunnels and mines are not damaged by earthquakes?

_____

_____

11. Read lines 118–121.

    a. What is the job of the Office of the U.S. Nuclear Waste Negotiator?

            _____

            _____

    b. In this sentence, **charged with** means

        1. to be made to pay for something
        2. to be suspected of a crime
        3. to be given responsibility for something

12. Read lines 121–126.

    a. What are some of the **incentives** David Leroy may offer?

            _____

    b. What are some of the **assurances** David Leroy may offer?

            _____

    c. An **incentive** is a

        1. guarantee
        2. motivation
        3. freedom

    d. An **assurance** is a

        1. guarantee
        2. motivation
        3. freedom

    e. **To lure** means to

        1. attract
        2. buy
        3. discourage

    f. **The sky is the limit** means

        1. he won't agree to build airplanes
        2. he will agree to construct tall buildings
        3. anything is possible

D. DICTIONARY SKILLS

Read the entry for each word and consider the context of the sentence from the passage. Write the number of definition that is appropriate for the context on the line next to the word. **Write the entry number, too, when appropriate.** Be prepared to explain your choice.

Part 1

1. With regard to incentives, such as highways, airports, schools, or harbor cleanups, David Leroy said, "You tell me what the problem is, and let's see if we can **address** it."

   address: _____

   > **ad·dress** \ə-'dres, a- *also* 'a-ˌdres\ *vb* [ME, *adressen*, fr, MF *adresser,* fr. *a-* (fr. L *ad-*) + *dresser* to arrange — more at DRESS] *vt* (14c) **1** *archaic* **a :** DIRECT, AIM **b :** to direct to go : SEND **2 a :** to direct the efforts or attention of (oneself) ⟨will ~ himself to the problem⟩ **b :** to deal with : TREAT ⟨intrigued by the chance to ~ important issues — I. L. Horowitz⟩ **3** *archaic* : to make ready; *esp* : DRESS **4 a :** to communicate directly ⟨~*es* his thank to his host⟩ **b :** to speak or write directly to; *esp* : to deliver a formal speech to **5 a :** to mark directions for delivery on ⟨~ a letter⟩ **b :** to consign to the care of another (as an agent or factor) **6 :** to greet by a prescribed form **7 :** to adjust the club preparatory to hitting (a golf ball) **8 :** to identify (as a peripheral or memory location) by an address or a name for information transfer ~ *vi, obs*: to direct one's speech or attentions — **ad·dress·er** *n*

\ə\abut \ᵊ\ kitten, \ər\ further \a\ ash \ā\ ace \ä\ mop, mar \aů \ out \ch\ chin \e\ bet \ē \ easy \g\go \i\ hit \ī\ ice \j\job \ŋ\sing \ō\ go \ȯ\ law \ȯi\ boy \th\ thin \t̲h̲\ the \ü\ loot \u̇\ foot \y\ yet \zh\ vision \à, k̲, ⁿ, œ, œ̄, ᵫ, ᵫ̄, ʸ\ *See Website below for* Pronunciation Guide.

By permission. From *Merriam-Webster's Online Dictionary* ©2002 by Merriam-Webster, Incorporated (www.Merriam-Webster.com).

2. Experts view Yucca Mountain, which is an arid, **desolate** ridge, as a good spot for a permanent nuclear graveyard.

desolate: _____

> **des·o·late** \\'de-sə-lət, 'de-zə-\\ _adj_ [ME, _desolat,_ fr. L _desolatur,_ pp. of _desolare_ to abandon, fr. _de-_ + _solus_ alone] (14c) **1 :** devoid of inhabitants and visitors : DESERTED **2 :** joyless, disconsolate, and sorrowful through or as if through separation from a loved one **3 a :** showing the effects of abandonment and neglect : DILAPIDATED **b :** BARREN, LIFELESS ⟨a ~ landscape⟩ **c :** devoid of warmth, comfort, or hope : GLOOMY ⟨~ memories⟩ _syn_ see ALONE — **des·o·late·ly** _adv_ — **des·o·late·ness** _n_

3. The Office of the U.S. Nuclear Waste Negotiator is charged with finding a willing state or Indian tribe to be a **host** for the repository.

host: _____

> **¹host** \\'hōst\\ _n_ [ME, fr. OF, fr. LL _hostis,_ fr. L, stranger, enemy — more at GUEST] (14c) **1 :** ARMY **2 :** a very large number : MULTITUDE
> **²host** _vi_ (15c) : to assemble in a host usu. for a hostile purpose
> **³host** _n_ [ME _hoste_ host, guest, fr. OF, fr. L _hospit-, hospes,_ prob. fr. _hostis_] (14c) **1 a :** one that receives or entertains guests socially, commercially, or officially **b :** one that provides facilities for an event or function ⟨our college served as ~ for the basketball tournament⟩ **2 a :** a living animal or plant affording subsistence or lodgment to a parasite **b :** the larger, stronger, or dominant member of a commensal or symbiotic pair **c :** an individual into which a tissue, part, or embryo is transplanted from another **3 :** a mineral or rock that is older than the minerals or rocks in it; _also_ : a substance that contains a usu. small amount of another substance incorporated in its structure **4 :** a radio or television emcee **5 :** a computer that controls communications in a network that administers a database

4. Thousands of tons of highly radioactive **spent** fuel rods rest temporarily today in pools of water near nuclear power plants around the country.

spent: _____

> **spent** \'spent\ *adj* [ME, fr. pp. of *spenden* to spend] (15c) **1 a :** used up : CONSUMED **b :** exhausted of active or required components or qualities often for a particular purpose ⟨~ nuclear fuel⟩ **2 :** drained of energy or effectiveness : EXHAUSTED **3 :** exhausted of spawn or sperm ⟨a ~ salmon⟩

Part 2

Sometimes a word not only has different meanings; it also has different pronunciations depending on the meaning. For example, in this chapter, the words **minute** and **refuse** each have several meanings and two different pronunciations. Read the entries for these words carefully and choose the most appropriate definition for the context. Check with your teacher to make sure that you pronounce the words correctly, depending on the meaning.

5. The possibility of a direct hit by an earthquake, and a new upwelling of magma right beneath the repository, is **minute,** according to scientists.

minute: _____

> **¹min·ute** \'mi-nət\ *n* [ME, fr. MF, fr. LL *minuta*, fr. L *minutus* small, fr. pp. of *minuere* to lessen — more at MINOR] (14c) **1 :** a 60th part of an hour of time or of a degree: 60 seconds **2 :** the distance one can traverse in a minute **3 :** a short space of time : MOMENT **4 a :** a brief note (as of summary or recommendation) **b :** MEMORANDUM, DRAFT **c** *pl* **:** the official record of the proceedings of a meeting
> **²minute** *vt* **min·ut·ed; min·ut·ing** (ca. 1648): to make notes or a brief summary of
> **³mi·nute** \mī-'nüt, mə-, -'nyüt\ *adj*
> **mi·nut·er; -est** [L *minutus*] (ca. 1626) **1 :** very small : INFINITESIMAL **2 :** of small importance : TRIFLING **3 :** marked by close attention to details *syn* see SMALL, CIRCUMSTANTIAL — **mi·nute·ness** *n*

6. The U.S. government plans to bury the nation's high-level nuclear **refuse** inside Yucca Mountain in Nevada.

   By the year 2,000, the nation will have produced 48,000 tons of high-level nuclear waste. Every speck of this **refuse** is intensely poisonous.

refuse: _____

¹**re·fuse** \ri-'fyüz\ *vb* **re·fused; re·fus·ing** [ME, fr. MF *refuser,* fr. (assumed) VL *refusare,* perh. blend of L *refutare* to refute and *recusare* to demur — more at RECUSE] *vt* (14c) **1 :** to express oneself as unwilling to accept ⟨~ a gift⟩ ⟨~ a promotion⟩ **2 a :** to show or express unwillingness to do or comply with ⟨*refused* to answer the question⟩ **b :** DENY ⟨they were *refused* admittance to the game⟩ **3** *obs* **:** GIVE UP, RENOUNCE **4** *of a horse* **:** to decline to jump or leap over ~ *vi* : to withhold acceptance, compliance, or permission *syn* see DECLINE — **re·fus·er** *n*
²**ref·use** \'re-'fyüs, -ˌfyüz\ *n* [ME, fr. MF *refus* rejection, fr. OF, fr. *refuser*] (14c) **1 :** the worthless or useless part of something : LEAVINGS **2 :** TRASH, GARBAGE
³**ref·use** \'re-ˌfyüs, -ˌfyüz\ *adj* (15c) : thrown aside or left as worthless

E. *Critical Thinking*

Read each question carefully. Write your response in the space provided. Remember that there is no one correct answer. Your response depends on what **you** think.

1. Does Betsy Carpenter, the author of this article, believe that there are sufficient reasons for not using Yucca Mountain as a nuclear waste site? Explain your answer.

   _____

   _____

   _____

2. Jerry Szymanski, who is a geologist, and "a number of earth scientists, also geologists," disagree on the interpretation of the same evidence, i.e., the calcite veins in the bedrock of Yucca Mountain. Why might Nevadans be unhappy with these conflicting interpretations of the same data?

   _____

   _____

   _____

3. According to the article, "The repository site must be capable of isolating atomic waste for 10,000 years," the length of time the waste material remains radioactive. What implications might you draw from this concern that the site remain intact for the full 10,000 years that it remains contaminated?

   _____

   _____

   _____

4. Does the government believe that most people would be willing to have a nuclear repository in their state? Explain your answer.

   _____

   _____

   _____

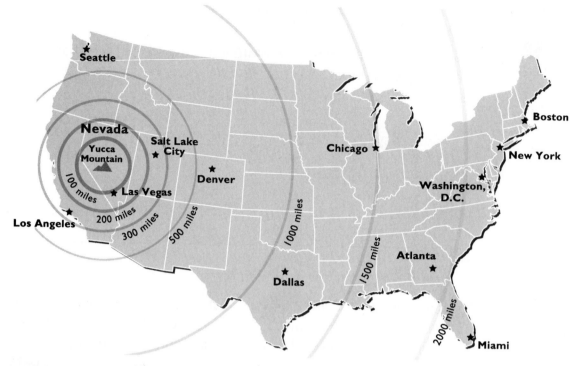

Another Perspective

A Nuclear Graveyard (excerpt)

1   The biggest problem at Yucca Mountain may be local opposition fomented in part by federal mishandling of the site-selection process. Nine years ago, Congress passed the Nuclear Waste Policy Act. In 1983, the DOE selected nine sites around the country for consideration as a possible repository. A couple of

5   years later, the list was narrowed down to three—Yucca Mountain, Hanford, Washington, and Deaf Smith County, Texas. Then, in 1987, Congress ordered the DOE to focus solely on Yucca Mountain, a move that Nevadans feel was made for political reasons: Nevada has one of the smallest delegations on Capitol Hill.[1] Today, anti-dump sentiment runs deep. Fully four out of five Nevadans oppose

10   the project.

Nevadans are also unnerved by the DOE's horrible environmental record and long-standing culture of secrecy. Indeed, billions of gallons of radioactive and toxic materials were dumped secretly over the past few decades at weapons factories around the country. According to a recent report by the Congressional

[1]Capitol Hill, in Washington, D.C., is the site of the Capitol building, where Congress, consisting of the Senate and the House of Representatives, meets to make laws. The number of representatives each state has is based on its population so that the least populated states have the fewest representatives and consequently, less voice in the House.

Office of Technology Assessment, the DOE's two-year-old effort to clean up the mess left on and under DOE weapons facilities is proceeding abysmally.

Changing Benchmarks

In their own defense, DOE officials argue that it is unfair to judge past practices by today's more stringent environmental standards. Moreover, they say the Yucca Mountain project has many layers of external oversight, unlike the weapons facilities that were cloaked in secrecy from the start. The DOE has a point. Every aspect of site evaluation will be scrutinized by the Nuclear Waste Technical Review Board, a panel of experts recommended by the National Academy of Sciences and appointed by the President. Ultimately, the facility will be licensed by the U.S. Nuclear Regulatory Commission.

But Nevadans have a case when they argue that their state has much to lose and little to gain by hosting the site. With its booming economy, Las Vegas doesn't need the 3,000 jobs the facility would provide during construction. Also, a nuclear accident, even a minor one, could harm the Silver State's gaming-based economy by keeping tourists away.

Many critics believe that the very notion of a site that could be "safe" for 10,000 years is ridiculous, and this has intensified local opposition. Science simply cannot prove that a site will be safe for such a long period of time, and citizens know it and feel as if they are being conned, says Frank Parker, chairman of the National Academy of Sciences' Board of Radioactive Waste Management. Parker holds that a more honest—and in the end more reassuring—assessment that the government could have offered Nevadans is that the likelihood of a catastrophic breach is very slim and that the DOE is prepared to act swiftly if problems occur.

1. According to Nevadans, why was Yucca Mountain chosen as the best site for the repository? What does the author imply when she says that Nevada has one of the smallest delegations on Capitol Hill?

   _____

   _____

   _____

2. Why do many people in Nevada oppose the dumping of nuclear waste in that state? What are their concerns?

   _____

   _____

   _____

3. How has the DOE said it would handle the Yucca Mountain situation differently than it handled other projects (for example, weapons facilities) in the past?

   _____

   _____

   _____

4. What business does the economy of Nevada depend on? How might this business be affected by nuclear dumping?

   _____

   _____

   _____

Follow-up Activities

1. Refer to the **Self-Evaluation of Reading Strategies** on the next page. Think about the strategies you used to help yourself understand "A Nuclear Graveyard." Check off the strategies you used. Evaluate your strategy use throughout the book. Which strategies have you begun to use consistently? Which strategies have you added to the list? Which strategies are becoming automatic? To what extent have you applied these strategies to other reading you do?

SELF-EVALUATION OF READING STRATEGIES

Strategies	Readings		
	"Playing with Fire"	"Wilder Places for Wild Things"	"A Nuclear Graveyard"
I read the title and try to predict what the reading will be about.			
I use my knowledge of the world to help me understand the text.			
I read as though I *expect* the text to have meaning.			
I use illustrations to help me understand the text.			
I ask myself questions about the text.			
I use a variety of types of context clues.			
I take chances in order to identify meaning.			
I continue if I am not successful.			
I identify and underline main ideas.			
I connect details with main ideas.			
I summarize the reading in my own words.			
I skip unnecessary words.			
I look up words correctly in the dictionary.			
I connect the reading to other material I have read.			
I do not translate into my native language.			

2. Look carefully at the illustration below. Read the sentences describing how a nuclear reactor operates. Then match the sentences to the appropriate letter in the illustration.

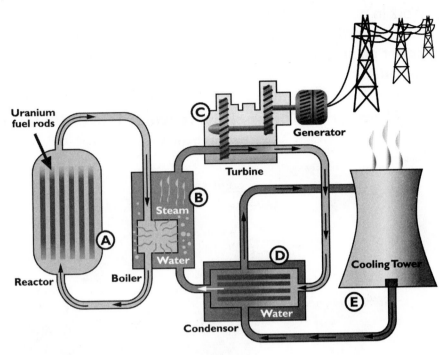

Operation of a Typical Nuclear Power Plant

_____ Hot coolant is piped through the boiler, where it heats water to steam.

_____ Steam drives the turbine, which generates electricity.

_____ In the cooling tower, water is cooled in air, recovered, and pumped through the condenser.

_____ In the reactor core, the radioactive fuel rods generate high temperatures, superheating a liquid coolant.

_____ Steam from the turbine is cooled back to water in the condenser, where it is recycled for use as steam.

3. Work in two groups. If your class is large, divide into an even number of groups. The first group will represent the Office of the U.S. Nuclear Waste Negotiator. This group will make a list of incentives and assurances to convince the other group to allow the government to build a nuclear repository in their state. The second group will represent the citizens of the state where the government wants to bury nuclear waste. This group will make a list of their concerns and demands. When the lists are completed, the students from both groups will discuss how to negotiate and compromise so that both groups are satisfied.

H. Topics for Discussion AND Writing

1. Work in pairs or small groups. Look carefully at the following chart. What observations can you make about the number and location of nuclear power plants throughout the world? Write a composition describing your conclusions.

Number of Commercial Nuclear Power Plants
(by continent)

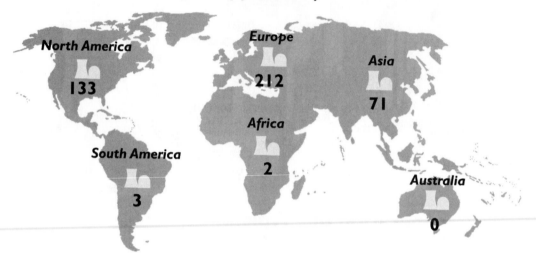

North America
133

Europe
212

Asia
71

Africa
2

South America
3

Australia
0

Antarctica
0

as of December 1993

2. If the government wanted to bury a nuclear repository in your state or province, how would you feel? Why? Write a letter to the editor of your local newspaper either in favor of or against the government's proposal.

3. In what other ways can governments dispose of nuclear waste? Discuss your ideas with your class. When you are finished, write a composition. Which ideas do you think are best? Explain your viewpoint.

4. **Write in your journal.** Do you think that the disposal of nuclear waste should be the responsibility of an individual country, or do you think this is a global issue? Explain your reasons. You may also want to discuss whether *all* environmental issues, including the destruction of rain forests, are the joint concern of all countries.

Cloze Quiz

Chapter 12: A Nuclear Graveyard

Read the passage below. Fill in the blanks with one word from the list. Use each word only once.

assurances	geologist	lure	radioactive	road
buried	government	Nevada	refuse	site
earthquakes	host	nuclear	remoteness	water
finding	incentives	poisonous	repository	years

The state of Nevada is fighting the federal government's plan to bury all

the nation's high-level nuclear _____ inside Yucca Mountain. But
(1)

in fact, the risk to Nevadans may be overstated. Increasingly, experts view this

arid, desolate ridge as a good spot for a permanent _____
(2)

graveyard. The threat to Americans posed by the federal government's

bungled attempts to find a safe burial _____ for the waste looms
(3)

large, however. Thousands of tons of highly _____ spent fuel
(4)

rods rest temporarily today in pools of _____ near nuclear
(5)

power plants around the country.

The twin virtues of the Yucca Mountain site are its _____
(6)

and aridity. From the summit, the only sign of civilization is the dusty trace of

a dirt _____ cutting across a brown, barren valley. The ridge is
(7)

located on the southwest corner of the Nevada Test Site, where the

_____ explodes nuclear weapons, so access is tightly restricted.
(8)

The landscape also provides stark reminders of why critics are so

concerned. To the southeast stands Busted Butte, a peak that was sheared in

half long ago by _____; to the west, four smooth-sloped
(9)

volcanoes rise out of a high valley. The reason for the geological turmoil is that immense forces inside the earth are stretching the earth's crust apart here. Earthquakes relieve the strain, but they also disrupt the water table.

The _____ (10) site must be capable of isolating atomic waste for 10,000 _____ (11). By all accounts, there could be a frightful mess if the poisons escaped the site. In a few years, the nation will have produced 48,000 tons of high-level nuclear waste, the most concentrated products of the nuclear era. Every speck of this refuse is intensely _____ (12).

Water is the worst enemy of _____ (13) nuclear waste. If water did find its way into the repository, it would corrode the storage canisters and hasten the escape of radioactive particles through the rock. Scientists cannot know absolutely whether ground water will well up under Yucca Mountain during the next 10,000 years.

"From what we know now, I would feel quite comfortable with Yucca Mountain," says George Thompson, a _____ (14) at Stanford University and a member of the National Academy of Sciences' panel. Though panel members agree that a lot more study is needed, most do not believe that the geological complexity disqualifies the site.

Congress must have had an inkling in 1987 that forcing the project on _____ (15) might not work out in the end. In the same bill that designated Yucca Mountain the sole candidate for site evaluation, Congress established the Office of the U.S. Nuclear Waste Negotiator, which is charged with _____ (16) a willing state or Indian tribe to _____ (17) the repository. David Leroy, who took the job last summer, is putting together a package of _____ (18) and assurances that he hopes will _____ (19) several state or tribal leaders to the bargaining table. The _____ (20) include promises of local participation in deciding how the facility is operated and the freedom to back out of the evaluation process at any time.

Unit 4 Review

Crossword Puzzle

Read the clues on the next page. Write the answers in the correct spaces in the puzzle.

Crossword Puzzle Clues

Across

1. Each; every
4. The opposite of **no**
6. Attract
8. An organized effort to promote or attain an end
10. I've lost a diamond earring. I am going to _____ the house until I find it.
12. A storage site is a _____
15. Susan waved her hand as a _____, or signal, for Ann to come into the room.
16. The grocer has some _____ fruit and vegetables. They have just been delivered.
18. John's house is in a very _____ location. I would not want to be so distant from other people.
21. Mountain lion; puma
22. Imitate closely
23. Research; carefully examine
24. Increase greatly in number
25. Deserted
26. Not paying attention
27. Do something as a favor

Down

1. Guarantee
2. The company used explosives to _____ the buildings. The whole area became very flat.
3. Provoke; cause something
5. Engross; absorb
7. An elephant
9. The opposite of **on**
11. The destruction of a forest
13. Used up; consumed
14. Exaggerate; make something seem larger than it is
17. Something that is about to happen is _____.
19. A motivation
20. There is a lot of _____ in the newspaper today. Some reporters made many exaggerated statements!

1. What is the role of modern zoos? Is it primarily entertainment? Education? Preservation of species? What are some ways that modern zoos are different from traditional ones?

2. Read the statements below and then watch the video once or twice. Decide whether each sentence is **True (T), False (F),** or an **Opinion (O).**

   A. _____ Ivan was captured when he was a young adult.

   B. _____ It was not unusual for gorillas to be confined in places like shopping malls 33 years ago.

   C. _____ Willie B., the silver-back gorilla, has a daughter named Kudzu.

   D. _____ Ivan will also become a father at Zoo Atlanta just as Willie B. did.

   E. _____ Zoo Atlanta's breeding program hasn't been successful yet.

3. In many modern zoos, people are confined inside, and animals are free to roam outside. Do you agree that "Turnabout is fair play"? Why or why not? Do you believe animals in modern zoos are comfortable and happy? Give evidence to support your opinion.

Find articles about endangered species by typing in "zoos and endangered species" and "endangered species of animals" in the InfoTrac College Edition online library. Skim the titles of the articles and choose a few about a particular animal (for example, the giant panda or the tiger) or a country or region you are interested in (for example, China or Europe) and the endangered animals that live there. Read several articles on the subject you chose. **Write a journal entry or short report** about what is being done to save the endangered species that you read about. Will those species continue to dwindle, or will new methods of saving and breeding them help them to proliferate once again?

INDEX OF KEY WORDS AND PHRASES

heritage 39, 218
high-stakes 192
hints 25
hostile 51
hype 231
hypothesis 79, 264

I
immerse 51, 240
immersion 242
imminent 218, 253
impoverished 170
in any event 149
inattention 218
incentive 266
incidental 112
incompatibility 26
incompatible 190
indifferent 51
indignantly 39
ingratiate 112
instrumental 53
interact 5
internship 148
irreversible 220
irreversibly 161

J
jeopardize 99

K
key 78, 219
kidney 148, 167–172, 192
kin 52, 171
kindle 3

L
landmark 77
last 50, 52, 169, 190, 192, 217, 230, 231, 240, 241, 266
launched 89, 190
lethal 148
leukemia 190
life span 88, 89
link 50, 52, 78, 99

lobes 203
logic 118
longevity 77, 78, 79
lose face 26
lure 266

M
maintained 148
malady 160
malignancy 100
marrow 190–192
martyr 172
master 120
mate 240
mediator 65
middle-born 64, 65
mimic 241
mindful 100, 101
mindfully 99
mindfulness 101
mindless 100
mindlessly 99
mindset 99, 100
minute 240
moratorium 3
moreover 218, 219, 279
mountain lion 252, 253
mounted 27

N
natural 240, 241
naturalistic 240, 242
naturalness 240
nature 112, 242
negotiator 65, 266
next of kin 171
notions 99
nuance 118
nuclear 263, 264, 265, 278, 279
nuclear waste 263, 264, 266, 278, 279

O
oblige 242
offspring 241, 242
on the outs 65

SKILLS INDEX

LISTENING/SPEAKING

Discussion, 2, 19, 20, 23, 24, 45, 69, 93, 94, 98, 114, 115, 136–137, 138, 143, 146, 163, 164, 184, 185, 207, 208, 235, 257, 263, 283, 284

Group activities, 2, 19, 20, 23, 24, 45, 69, 77, 93, 94, 98, 114, 115, 136–137, 138, 143, 146, 163, 164, 168, 184, 185, 207, 208, 234, 235, 256, 257, 263, 283, 284

Interviewing, 19, 41, 68, 234, 256

Partner activities, 19, 41, 68, 93, 114

Reports, 77

Role playing, 114

Surveys, 24, 49, 68, 93, 168, 207

READING

Charts, 43–44, 77, 91–93, 183–184, 233–234

Critical thinking strategies, 15, 36–37, 63, 87, 110, 131–132, 158–159, 181–182, 202, 228–229, 251, 277

Details, 8, 28, 55–56, 81, 102–103, 124, 150–151, 173–174, 194, 221–222, 244–245, 267

Dictionary skills, 13–14, 33–35, 60–62, 85–86, 108–109, 129–130, 156–157, 178–180, 200–201, 226–227, 249–250, 273–276

Follow-up activities, 19, 41–44, 66–68, 91–93, 114, 136–137, 163, 182–184, 205–207, 233–234, 256, 281–283

Main ideas, 7, 28, 54, 80, 102, 123, 150, 173, 193, 221, 244, 267

Outlines, 221–222, 244–245

Prereading activities, 2, 23, 49, 76, 97, 118, 146, 167, 188, 216, 239, 261

Reading analysis, 10–12, 31–32, 58–59, 83–84, 106–107, 127–128, 154–155, 176–177, 197–199, 224–225, 247–248, 270–272

Self-evaluation of reading strategies, 137, 206, 282

Statement evaluation, 9, 30, 57, 74, 82, 105, 126, 153, 175, 196, 223, 246, 269

TECHNOLOGY-INTERNET

INFOTRAC research activities, 74, 144, 214, 290

TEST-TAKING SKILLS

Cloze quizzes, 21–22, 46–48, 70–71, 95–96, 116–117, 139–140, 165–166, 186–187, 209–210, 236–238, 258–260, 285–286

Matching, 283

Multiple-choice questions, 10–12, 31–32, 58, 59, 83, 84, 106, 107, 127, 128, 154–155, 176–177, 197, 198–199, 224, 225, 247, 262, 270, 271, 272
Short-answer questions, 10, 11, 12, 15, 18, 31, 32, 36–37, 40, 43–44, 54, 58, 59, 63, 66, 80, 83, 84, 87, 90, 91–93, 106–107, 110, 113, 123, 127, 128, 131–132, 150, 154, 155, 158–159, 162, 173, 176, 177, 181–182, 183–184, 188–189, 193, 197, 198, 202, 204, 217, 224, 225, 228–229, 232, 234, 244, 247, 251, 254, 270, 271–272, 280

TOPICS
Assisted suicide, 146–166
Child prodigies, 118–140
Computers in classrooms, 2–22
Health, 97–117
Longevity, 76–96
Mixed marriage, 23–48
Naturalistic zoos, 239–260
Nuclear waste, 261–286
Organ transplants, 188–210
Rain forests, 216–238
Selling human organs, 167–187
Siblings, 49–71

VIEWING
Photographs, 2, 97
Video reports, 74, 143, 213, 289

WRITING
Charts, 2, 8, 24, 28, 29, 41, 42, 49–50, 67, 68, 76, 77, 81, 102–103, 119, 124, 135, 137, 150–151, 173–174, 206, 207, 239, 262, 267, 282
Crossword puzzles, 72–73, 141–142, 211–212, 287–288
Definitions, 119
Group activities, 2, 23, 97–98, 119, 146, 163, 239, 256, 283
Journals, 20, 24, 45, 69, 74, 94, 115, 138, 144, 164, 185, 208, 235, 257, 284, 290
Lists, 2, 23, 97–98, 136–137, 146, 163, 184, 256, 263, 283
Outlines, 55–56, 173–174
Partner activities, 136–137, 146, 163, 217, 262
Reports, 77, 144
Summaries, 8, 28, 29, 55, 56, 81, 102, 104, 124, 125, 150, 152, 173, 174, 194, 195, 221, 222, 244, 245, 267, 268